A Chronology of the American Revolution in North Carolina

A List of Dates in a National and International Context

ISBN 978-0-8652-6515-8

Typefaces used in this book are Adobe Caslon Pro, LTC Fleurons, and P22 1722 Pro.

Cover illustration: The Battle of Guilford Courthouse was the largest and most important of the Revolutionary War battles fought in North Carolina. Cornwallis finally caught up with Greene's army and attempted a decisive clash to destroy the Continental Army in the South. Greene arranged his force in successive lines, similar to Morgan's deployment at Cowpens. Cornwallis attacked and drove back the first two Patriot lines, but the fighting became more intense at the third line. Eventually Greene was forced to withdraw, but Cornwallis's army lost twenty-seven percent of its numbers, either killed or wounded, wrecking its effectiveness (also on p. 159). Painting by Don Troiani, courtesy of Bridgeman Images.

Distributed by the University of North Carolina Press.

CONTENTS

Introduction

Two hundred and fifty years ago, Britain's North American colonists were locked in a political struggle with the British government regarding their rights within the imperial system. Parliament introduced a series of taxation laws, intended to pay for the support of British troops stationed in the colonies. The colonists assumed they had the same rights as Englishmen in England and believed they should not be taxed without some form of direct representation. The British government argued that Parliament represented the interests of the colonists despite a lack of direct representatives sitting within that legislative body. The conflict escalated, with neither side truly understanding the position of the other. Colonial opponents of the British policies resorted to violence and intimidation to achieve their goals, which resulted in stronger pushback from Britain, whose leaders and people began to view the colonists as rebels and traitors. Fighting between colonial militia and British troops began in April 1775. A little over a year later, in July 1776, the Continental Congress, created to act as a governing body for the united colonies as British authority collapsed, declared the colonies independent of Britain and joined together in a new nation, the United States.

Declaring independence was not the same thing as having it, however, as Britain was determined to repress the rebellion and return the colonies to the fold. Britain was motivated by the potential loss of power and prestige among the other powerful European colonial empires if it lost control of the North American colonies. The British also believed that the majority of American colonists remained loyal to the monarchy and had only been manipulated by unscrupulous radical political leaders. A few British victories would bring them to their senses. While there were many living in the colonies who expressed loyalty to Britain, their numbers were never as large as the faraway British government believed. Of those who supported Britain, only a comparative few were willing to risk everything to openly enlist and fight in the British cause, especially in the face of repressive measures by the state militias to keep them in line. However, Britain possessed the advantage of a well-trained army and a large fleet, while the rebellious colonists had to create both an army and navy from scratch and instill the military discipline necessary to successfully defeat the British.

The British army in America initially gained the upper hand and beat the rebel armies repeatedly, yet they never completely destroyed them. Following the American victory at Saratoga in 1777, the conflict shifted from a war in which Britain sought to regain its rebellious colonies into a major international conflict. France, Britain's traditional major foe among the great European powers, had long been involved in illegally supplying the rebels with the assistance of Spain and the Netherlands. The French decided largely on the basis of Saratoga, that the rebellious Americans, or Patriots, had a chance of winning, and forged a formal military and commercial alliance with the United States in 1778. Spain, another longtime foe of Britain and ally of the French, joined the war in 1779. In 1780, Britain declared war against its former ally, the Netherlands, in exasperation over the officially covert but far from secret assistance that the Dutch had been giving to the Patriots. Neither Spain nor the Netherlands formerly allied with the Patriots, but the enlarged conflict strained British military and naval resources to the maximum. Britain now had to defend its territories around the globe, and even Britain itself, from a possible invasion by the French. At the same time, Britain's war aims expanded as it sought not only to defend its empire but expand it, targeting French, Spanish, and Dutch colonial possessions, especially in the Caribbean and in India.

As a result, the British reduced their military and naval commitments to suppress the rebellion in North America. The goal to reconquer the colonies was not abandoned, but the British commanders in North America were expected to do more with less, as troops and ships were transferred to other parts of the conflict. Out of this situation was born what became known as "the Southern Strategy," the plan to reconquer the colonies, or at least the part most economically important to Britain, by launching a major military campaign in that region. Initiated partly due to the belief in the British government that the White population of the South was dominated by people still loyal to the Crown, the plan was for British troops to conquer South Carolina first, followed by efforts to raise and enlist the Loyalists and turn over control to them while the British moved on into North Carolina and repeated the process. If successful, it was hoped that Virginia and Maryland would be added; Georgia, which already had British troops operating in its territory, would be brought completely under British control. Beside the expected overwhelming cooperation of the Loyalist population, the British also hinged much of their strategy on the assistance of their Indian allies on the frontier. With the organization of the Loyalists into military units and the cooperation of the Indians, the British would accomplish their goals with the use of fewer regular troops. Britain's ultimate plan was a single block of connected territory, ranging from East and West Florida in the South (already under British control) to the Chesapeake in the mid-Atlantic, which could then be used as a launching point to reconquer the North or compel a peace agreement on their terms. Even if the rest of the United States retained its independence, it would be a politically and economically weak nation surrounded by British territory on all sides.

Unfortunately for the British, the Southern Strategy was based on a number of false assumptions. While Loyalism was stronger in the South than in other parts of the United States, it did not make up a majority of the population anywhere. Furthermore, after years of neglect from the British and ruthless repression by Patriot state governments, they were reluctant to rise up and organize to fight for the British, unless a strong British military presence was maintained in their respective states. In other words, a successful Loyalist uprising required the commitment of more British troops to the fighting in North America, rather than less. The Indians, already battered by years of devastating Patriot expeditions into their territories, also did not turn out in the numbers that the British hoped. As a result, the Southern Strategy was in trouble from the moment it began.

The British campaign to reconquer the South began in 1780, with the capture of Charleston, South Carolina, by an army under the command of British commander-in-chief in North America Sir Henry Clinton. The British soon expanded outward and gained control of much of the state's interior. Clinton then departed for New York City, where the bulk of his army was located, and left the Southern expeditionary force under his subordinate, Charles, Earl Cornwallis. Cornwallis prepared to move into North Carolina, even though he soon discovered that the British control of southern and central South Carolina was tentative. Outside of the various posts where British troops were stationed, Patriot guerilla forces operated in the interior, hitting British posts, patrols, and foraging parties and disrupting communications and supply lines. Expeditions sent to suppress the guerillas achieved mixed results at best. Nevertheless, Cornwallis did not alter his plans, particularly after he crushed the Patriot regular army in the South under Horatio Gates, the hero of Saratoga, in August at Camden. Cornwallis's march northward brought him as far as Charlotte, but he was forced to retreat to South Carolina when Patriot "Overmountain Men" virtually annihilated his flanking column at Kings Mountain, South Carolina in October.

Nathanael Greene, a veteran officer from Washington's army in the North, replaced Gates as commander of the Patriot army in the South. He began rebuilding the army while Cornwallis struggled unsuccessfully to suppress the guerillas in South Carolina. In December, Greene decided to solve the problem he faced in feeding his army by detaching a major portion under Daniel Morgan to forage in South Carolina. A British attempt to entrap Morgan led to a Patriot victory at Cowpens, South Carolina, in January 1781, a major turning point in the Southern campaign. Thereafter, Greene moved to unite his divided army and reach safety in Virginia as Cornwallis closely pursued. Crossing the flooded Dan River and taking all of the boats to prevent the British following, Greene's army was reinforced and in March moved back into North Carolina. Cornwallis, meanwhile, attempted to raise Loyalists for the British cause while his own army, far from its supply base in South Carolina, struggled to feed itself. Both commanders sought a decisive battle and clashed at Guilford Courthouse in March, the largest Revolutionary War battle fought in North Carolina. Cornwallis drove Greene off the field after a hard fight that cost a quarter of his own army.

Afterwards, the rival armies moved in opposite paths. Cornwallis initially sought refuge and resupply in Wilmington, while Greene decided to attack the various British posts in South Carolina. A frustrated Cornwallis chose not to follow, despite his instructions to secure South Carolina before advancing further. Instead, he marched his army from Wilmington into Virginia. While Greene gradually forced the British to abandon their various posts and concentrate at Charleston and Savannah, a joint American and French army under Washington and a French Fleet entrapped Cornwallis's army at Yorktown. The surrender of the British army at Yorktown in October 1781 marked the effective end of the war, although two years of negotiations and additional fighting around the globe transpired until the United States and Britain signed a peace treaty in Paris in September 1783, guaranteeing American independence.

Following the war, the leaders and citizens of the United States had much work to do in order to establish an effective nation. The country was governed by the Articles of Confederation, a document that established a weak central government and granted extensive powers to the original states. Many initially preferred this method of government, a natural reaction to the governing style of the British during the years leading up to the Revolution. But problems soon arose regarding issues of national policy, and there was much conflict between the individual states. An increasing number of influential political figures began to feel the Articles needed extensive revision, or replacement altogether. A convention of representatives from the states, organized to revise the Articles, met in Philadelphia in May 1787. Instead of a revision of the Articles, the convention produced a new governing document after months of debate and compromise.

Called the Constitution, the new document was sent to the states for ratification. Two major political factions soon coalesced in support for or against the Constitution. Those who supported the Constitution became known as the Federalists, while its critics were the Anti-Federalists. The latter favored the weaker government of the Articles of Confederation and strong state governments, and worried that the strong central government of the Constitution posed a potential threat to individual liberties. North Carolina initially sat in the Anti-Federalist camp, which led to it being one of two states temporarily out of the Union when the Constitution was ratified and adopted by the other states and the new government went into effect. The passage of the first ten amendments to the Constitution, known as the Bill of Rights, addressed many of the concerns of the Anti-Federalists, and North Carolina subsequently ratified the Constituation.

This chronology charts the course of the political disagreements which led to the Revolution, the events of the War for Independence, and the postwar period that led to the adoption of the Constitution. The focus will be on matters related directly to North Carolina, but some attention is paid to the bigger national and, in some cases, international picture to present developments in North Carolina in context.

Note on terminology: In British politics, the Whig faction supported a constitutional monarchy and a parliamentary system. The rival Tory faction supported a strong and dominant monarchy. During the crisis leading up to the American Revolution, those Americans who opposed British policies called themselves Whigs, as they supported the rights of their own colonial legislatures to decide taxation and other policies in parallel with British Whig support for a strong Parliament. This parallel conveniently ignored that the British Parliament was largely responsible for the policies to which American Whigs objected, albeit policies supported and often initiated by the king and the British cabinet ministry. Those "American Whigs" also called themselves Patriots. Once war broke out between the colonies and Britain in 1775, Americans who remained loyal to Britain became known as the Loyalists; however, the American Whigs or Patriots frequently referred to them as "Tories" after the Tory faction in Britain. In this text, distinctions will be made between American and British Whigs and Tories, although for convenience the terms Patriot and Loyalist will be used as much as possible. An effort has been made to not refer to people involved in the revolutionary movement as "the Americans" as much as possible regarding events prior to formal independence in 1783, given that there were many Americans who supported the British government or who sought to remain personally neutral, and that sometimes groups or individuals from, or associated with, other American communities, such as Native Americans and Spanish American colonials, were involved in the struggle.

Part I

The Establishment of North Carolina and Early English Regulation of Colonial Trade

After an early and unsuccessful effort to establish a colony in what is now North Carolina during the reign of Elizabeth I, King Charles II created a colony called Carolina in 1663. The province was the domain of a group of Lords Proprietor who played a role in the Restoration of Charles to the English monarchy following the chaos of the British Civil Wars, the execution of Charles I, and the short-lived Commonwealth which replaced the monarchy. The new colony was locally governed from Charles Town (modern Charleston, South Carolina). Much of the colony's economic strength was located in what is now the South Carolina lowcountry, where a plantation agriculture took root, based largely on rice and powered by the labors of enslaved people. Along the northern coast of the colony, settlement was sparser and included squatters from Virginia as well as immigrants coming directly from England and other parts of Europe. Settled communities took shape in this region beginning around the Albemarle Sound and gradually moved southward. Much of the economic activity of that region was based on tobacco cultivation and, later, naval stores.

Even before the colony of Carolina was established, England took its first steps to regulate trade in a series of measures that bore an increasingly negative economic impact on its North American colonies. Called the Navigation Acts, these laws intended to ensure England's control of its international trade by mandating that goods were carried to and from the country in English ships, thereby limiting the items that colonists could ship abroad to other countries. By the 1670s, discontent over the collection of duties in the northern part of Carolina led to Culpepper's Rebellion, one of the earliest uprisings in British North America and a distant forerunner of the unrest which led to the American Revolution.

October 9, 1651

The first Navigation Act was passed by the British Parliament. The act and its successors regulated trade between England and its colonies in favor of England. The navigation acts were based on the principle of mercantilism, an economic theory prevalent across Europe, which argued that exports should dominate a country's trade, with imports kept to the minimum. Under this system, colonies should export raw materials to their home country, which then would be fashioned into finished goods to be exported to other countries or to the colonies. Some agricultural products, such as tobacco, sugar, and rice would have duties (taxes) collected at every stage of the export/import process; such goods were referred to as "enumerated items." The primary target of this first act was the Dutch

Republic, which played a dominant role in European trade and over England's coastal transportation. The act required that goods imported from outside of Europe be transported in English vessels; the same would be true for goods imported from other European countries, with the exception that foreign vessels could bring to England goods produced by their own particular countries. Imported saltwater fish and fish oil were banned, and saltwater fish could only be exported in English ships. Foreign ships were prohibited from transporting goods from one English port to another. Penalties, including forfeiture of a vessel or cargo, would be imposed on violators. There were certain exceptions for goods shipped from the territory of the East India Company, shipments of bullion, shipments of silk or silk products from Italy, and goods imported from Spanish or Portuguese ports. The overall impact was to strengthen English shipping and transportation at the expense of foreign traders, and to protect the interests of the English fishing industry.

May–June 1660

The English government under Charles II organized the position of Secretary of State into two offices, each with its own secretary. By 1689, these would be known as the Secretary of State for the Northern Department and the Secretary of State for the Southern Department. Responsibilities for each department were divided geographically. The Southern Department was considered senior, and was responsible for affairs in southern England, Wales, Ireland, Britain's American colonies, and for foreign relations with the Catholic and Muslim countries of Europe. The Northern Department handled affairs in northern England, Scotland, and foreign relations with the Protestant countries of Europe.

September 13, 1660

The first of the royal Navigation Acts following the Restoration of the Monarchy was passed by Parliament, all laws passed previously by the Commonwealth having been repealed.

July 27, 1661

As the previous Parliament was an interim body that sat during the transition from the Commonwealth to the Restoration, it was disbanded by the king late in 1660 and a new Parliament called, which in 1661 confirmed the acts of its predecessor. On this date, the new Parliament confirmed the Navigation Act of 1660.

March 24, 1663

Charles II granted the original Carolina Charter to eight of his supporters, who became Lords Proprietor of the colony. Among its provisions was a seven-year moratorium on the collection of export duties on tobacco and other items.

July 27, 1663

Parliament passed a new Navigation Act (Encouragement of Trade Act of 1663/the Staple Act). European goods imported to British colonies were now required to be shipped to England first, unloaded, and after inspection and payment of duties, reloaded onto English or English colonial vessels for reshipment to their destinations. Likewise, enumerated items exported from the colonies, such as tobacco, had to be unloaded and duties on them paid before they could be transported elsewhere. Again, there were exemptions. The main goal and impact of the act was to place limits on colonial trade, and specifically prevent the colonies from developing their own transportation system. Shipment of goods was now firmly in the hands of England, with costs passed on to the colonists.

1670

The moratorium on export duties for the colony of Carolina ended, and the colonists had to comply with all provisions of the Navigation Acts regarding trade.

1672

Growing discontent among the residents of Albemarle County over the adverse economic impact of the Navigation Acts led the Assembly of Albemarle to dispatch Gov. Peter Carteret to England to consult with the Lords Proprietor. Carteret's mission was to convince the Proprietors not to collect the required duties. Worried that the king might revoke the charter if they did so, the Proprietors refused.

1677

Culpepper's Rebellion broke out in Albemarle County. The impetus was growing anger over the collection of customs. Albemarle resident Thomas Miller and Speaker of the Assembly Thomas Eastchurch were critics of acting governor John Jenkins, who practiced a very lax enforcement of the Navigation Acts. Miller was jailed for treason but escaped and went with Eastchurch to complain to the Proprietors. In response, the Proprietors appointed Eastchurch as governor and Miller as secretary of the colony and the collector. However, as most colonists opposed the Navigation duties, they objected to the new appointments. Miller returned to the province first, and proved to be an efficient and ruthless collector of the duties. He was also corrupt and jailed personal enemies, which sparked the rebellion. A group of some forty men, led by John Culpepper and two others, seized control of the government and arrested Miller and his associates. Eastchurch, who had only just recently arrived in Virginia on his way to Carolina, was warned not to come. The rebels held new elections for an assembly and then tried and convicted Miller. He escaped, however, and went to England to see the Proprietors. The rebels sent Culpepper to England as well to argue their case. Upon his arrival in England, Culpepper was arrested and tried for rebellion, but the Proprietors, who wished to keep matters out of the public eye due to the general lawlessness and lack of authority in the colony, acquitted him. Culpepper returned to Carolina to a hero's welcome. While the Proprietors resolved to administer their province more firmly, they did little to accomplish it. Along with Bacon's Rebellion in Virginia, 1676–1677, although the latter had very different causes, Culpepper's Rebellion demonstrated that conflict between colonists and their colonial overlords could lead to uprisings and violence.

Part II

International Conflict and the Background of the Revolution

Between 1688 and 1815 a series of wars were fought between Britain and France. The conflicts were largely driven by the concerns of various European powers, over time principally Britain, with French expansionism in Europe and the colonial world. The exception would be the American Revolutionary War, which began due to internal conflicts between Britain and its North American colonies but became an international conflict when the United States formed an alliance with France. In all of the conflicts except the American Revolutionary War, both Britain and France were part of large international alliances which included other European powers and, outside of Europe, indigenous powers and colonial dependencies. In the Revolutionary War, by contrast, the alliances were of a more limited nature. The principal military operations occurred in Europe in each of those wars except the American Revolutionary War, but fighting around the globe took place in all of them.

The wars in this cycle of conflict fought before the American Revolution were the Nine Years' War (1688–1697, known in British North America as King William's War); the War of the Spanish Succession (or Queen Anne's War, 1701–1714); two originally separate wars, the War of Jenkins' Ear (1739–1748) and the War of the Austrian Succession (1740–1748) that merged into a single conflict in 1744 (known as King George's War in British North America); and the Seven Years' War (1756–1763), which had unofficially began two years earlier in America (known there as the French and Indian War).

The Nine Years' War was entangled with the Glorious Revolution in England (November 1688), which saw James II of England (James VI of Scotland) deposed over fears that he would restore Catholicism as England's official religion, in favor of his Protestant daughter Mary and her husband and cousin, William of Orange, Stadtholder (ruler) of the Dutch Republic and leader of a European coalition opposed to the territorial ambitions of France's Louis XIV. Those ambitions transformed into reality when Louis invaded the western Holy Roman Empire in September 1688, marking the start of the Nine Years' War. France lost most of its European gains in the peace treaty and recognized William as the legitimate king of England. The War of the Austrian Succession erupted as a result of Louis's efforts to put a grandson on the throne of Spain, exciting fears of a unified Franco-Spanish empire. The peace treaty explicitly prohibited that from happening, although French and Spanish foreign policies were often in sync during succeeding conflicts due to the monarchs of both countries being from different branches of the same family. The War of Jenkins' Ear broke out due to British efforts to expand trade within zones dominated by Spain, and Spanish worries over Britain's growing colonial power in the Americas. The War of the Austrian Succession was primarily sparked by the growing rivalry between the powerful German states of Austria and Prussia and Prussia's ambitions to gain territory at Austria's expense. France joined the war against Austria, and Britain entered the war on Austria's side in 1744, with Spain allied to France. The peace treaty ended the fighting but did not resolve the causes of the conflict. The French and Indian War began in 1754 as a struggle between France and several British colonies in North America, principally over control of territory in what is now western Pennsylvania claimed by both empires. After a clash between Virginia militia and French forces that ended in a French victory, British troops became involved in the conflict, which waged undeclared for two years before war officially broke out in Europe in 1756. During the subsequent Seven Years' War, Britain battled France and Spain around the globe while Britain's major continental ally, Prussia, strengthened by British military subsidies, fought against France, Austria, Russia and other powers. Britain won major victories, including the conquest of what is now Canada, and became the most powerful nation in Europe, while Prussia avoided defeat after a series of campaigns that left its countryside devastated. Although Britain emerged from the war powerful and confident, it was also widely seen as arrogant and resented among the other European powers. In a more ominous development, Britain was left without any allies, as the Prussians felt betrayed when Britain ceased its military subsidies at a key point in the conflict.

Collectively, the four conflicts helped set the stage for the American Revolution in various ways. Britain's efforts to control its colonial trade became of increasing importance, but its territorial gains at the expense of its rivals led to the eventual entry of France and Spain against Britain in the Revolutionary War. During this period, Parliament passed Britain's Bill of Rights to become law, a source of future inspiration for the American revolutionaries and their views on their own rights as Englishmen.
In British North America, the Albany Congress of 1754 marked a failed effort to establish an inter-colony system of defense that later bore fruit in the colonial Committees of Correspondence and Safety and the Continental Congress.

The era brought change for the colony of Carolina as it split into North and South Carolina. The two new colonies continued to develop along the distinctive lines already established in the northern and southern parts of the previous single colony. Immigration increased to both Carolinas, leading not only to the founding of new communities and the growth of existing ones along the coast and in the eastern plain, but an increase of settlement in the backcountry, the area roughly corresponding with the modern-day Piedmont. The new arrivals included immigrants freshly arrived from overseas, as well as others who originally settled in the northern colonies and moved southward or whose descendants, after a generation or two, decided to do so. Those immigrants followed the Great Wagon Road from Pennsylvania down into the Shenandoah Valley of Virginia, North Carolina, South Carolina and, later in the century, Georgia. The enslaved population of the Carolinas also grew, as plantation agriculture continued to expand, particularly in the eastern part of the colonies which were more suited for large-scale agriculture than the backcountry.

The influx of new immigrants into the backcountry led to growing conflict between the colonists and the Indians. Two major wars erupted during the middle and late 1710s, the first with the Tuscarora and allied tribes in North Carolina and the Yamasee in South Carolina, while another war with the Cherokee would break out during the Seven Years' War. The settlers, sometimes with the help of British troops, ultimately emerged victorious in the struggles. Although the power of the eastern tribes was broken, the Cherokee still remained a powerful force in the southern British colonies for decades.

December 16, 1689

The English Bill of Rights of 1689 were given royal assent and became law. Resulting from the Glorious Revolution, the bill established the basic foundations of constitutional monarchy in England. Parliament was recognized as having primacy over the English crown, and guaranteed the right to meet annually, under free elections. Free speech was guaranteed for the legislative body as well. The principal of no taxation without representation in Parliament was established for English citizens residing in the home country but not in the colonies. It also granted a number of rights for individual citizens, including the prohibition of cruel and unusual punishment for those convicted of criminal offenses. The English Bill of Rights thus established some of the political ideology later used by the colonists in their struggle against Britain during the Revolution.

November 8, 1691

The Lords Proprietor instructed Carolina Gov. Philip Ludwell to appoint a deputy governor to administer Albemarle County, the northern part of the province of Carolina which corresponds to modern-day North Carolina. This began the process which led to the separation of Carolina into two separate provinces in 1712.

August 1695–October 29, 1696

John Archdale, a Quaker, was governor of Carolina during this period. His term was the apex of a period in which Quakers dominated the government of the province. The rise of a strong Anglican party within Carolina in succeeding years sparked conflict which eventually led to Cary's Rebellion in 1711.

1699–1704

Henderson Walker served as the acting deputy governor of Carolina during this period. He was never formally named to the position of deputy governor by the governor of Carolina in Charles Town but assumed the position on the death of Deputy Governor Thomas Harvey in Walker's capacity as President of the Executive Council of Carolina. A devout Anglican, Walker supported the monarchy in its conflicts with the Lords Proprietor and worked to formally establish the Church of England as the official denomination of the colony, although with limited success. His tenure marked the beginning of a "Church Party" within the provincial government that struggled with the "Quaker Party" for control.

1701

The colonial legislature passed the first Vestry Act, which made the Church of England the official denomination of the province of Carolina. There is no surviving copy of this act, and it is likely that the Lords Proprietor disallowed it. A similar act passed in 1711, which also did not survive and was also probably disallowed by the Proprietors. Although not fully implemented at this time, these early vestry acts paved the way for the foundation of an Anglican establishment which, although never as strong as in the portion of the province which became South Carolina, was the source of later conflict in the backcountry with settlers who belonged to other denominations.

November 10–December 30, 1702

English colonial forces and their Indian allies besieged St. Augustine, Florida, as part of the War of the Spanish Succession. The colonists and Indians were led by Col. James Moore, governor of the province of Carolina. There had been tensions between the two colonies since Carolina gained control of trade in the region, particularly the slave trade, and because of the Spanish policy of giving refuge to runaway slaves from Carolina who then converted to Catholicism. Even before the outbreak of war, there had been talk in Carolina of capturing the important Spanish post. Moore's forces arrived on November 10 to find St. Augustine deserted, as the colony's governor, José de Zúñiga y la Cerda, was aware that the expedition was coming and moved the citizens and supplies into the Castillo de San Marcos, the fortress that guarded the town. Moore's efforts to batter the masonry fortress into surrender proved unsuccessful, and the arrival of a Spanish relief force from Havana led to Moore's withdrawal.

1705–1708

During these years, Thomas Cary served as the deputy governor of Carolina. A native of England, Cary immigrated to Carolina and settled in the southern part of the colony (modern South Carolina). Appointed deputy governor to oversee the section of the colony that is now North Carolina, Cary soon became a supporter of the "Church Party" faction in Carolina government that favored the Anglican Church over the "Quaker Party." Cary enforced a parliamentary law that required office holders to swear an oath of allegiance to Queen Anne, which barred Quakers from serving in government as their religion forbids the swearing of oaths. The Quakers and other religious dissenters sent John Porter, an Anglican of Quaker descent, to England to present grievances against Cary to the Proprietors. Cary was elected in 1707 to the assembly for the southern part of the province and became its speaker. While serving in the assembly in Charles Town, he appointed William Glover to the post of acting deputy governor. Porter meanwhile was successful in his mission to the Proprietors and returned with orders to remove Cary from the post of deputy governor. Finding Glover acting in Cary's place, Porter oversaw the election of a new council for Albemarle Province, which in turn formally elected Glover to the post of deputy governor. However, Porter's instructions from the Proprietors required that Cary and the members of the former council be present in order for any new elections to have formal standing. Porter chose not to follow those instructions, and for the time they remained a secret.

May 1, 1707

The Kingdom of Great Britain was created by the formal merger of the kingdoms of England and Scotland, the result of acts passed by the English Parliament in 1706 and the Scottish Parliament in 1707. At this time, the country was still ruled by Anne, daughter of the deposed James II and sister of the late Queen Mary II. Among other provisions, the union led to the regulation of trade throughout the realm with the formerly English colonies.

1708–1711

The political situation in northern Carolina remained in turmoil. John Porter soon discovered that William Glover was no friend to the "Quaker Party" in Albemarle politics, requiring that officials under him swear oaths and thus continuing the disqualification of Quakers in office begun by Thomas Cary. Porter then tried to depose Glover, revealing for the first time the instructions requiring Cary and the former Council members to be present for the elections of a new deputy governor and members of the council to be legal, and thus argued that Glover's election was illegal. This was only the first twist in the struggle for power, for at this point Cary returned, allied himself with the Quakers and was restored to power as deputy governor. With his shift in allegiance to the "Quaker Party," Cary evidently acquired Porter's loyalty, as he served on Cary's Council. Glover, in the meantime, left Carolina for Virginia.

December 7, 1710

At a meeting in London, the Lords Proprietor decided to divide the colony of Carolina into two provinces, North Carolina and South Carolina. They made the decision for administrative reasons and the fact that the two sections were vastly different in settlement patterns and economies.

1711

Cary's Rebellion, an uprising in Albemarle Province, occurred in this year. Edward Hyde was appointed deputy governor of Carolina by the Proprietors in 1710 and arrived in North Carolina in January 1711. Initially his authority was accepted as legitimate by Thomas Cary and his supporters, even though Gov. Edward Tynte had died in June 1710 and thus Hyde's commission had not received a governor's signature. This situation played out against a background of conflict in Charles Town over the position of acting governor, as Robert Gibbes had received that position through the Executive Council by one vote over his opponent, Thomas Broughton, and that vote was the result of bribery. Armed conflict between the followers of Gibbes and Broughton soon followed. The Lords Proprietor eventually ruled Gibbes's election illegal due to the bribery, but they allowed him to continue in office until the arrival of his successor, Charles Craven, in March 1712. In the meantime, violence erupted in the northern part of the colony in the absence of a legitimated executive authority in Charles Town. The source of the conflict was the old struggle between the faction dominated by the Quakers and members of other dissenting sects, and the party that supported the establishment and the authority of the Anglican Church. Hyde allied himself with the latter soon after his arrival, and Cary withdrew his support from him, citing the lack of a gubernatorial signature on Hyde's commission and claiming that he himself was still acting deputy governor under his old authority. In March 1711, Hyde asked the assembly for the northern part of Carolina to pass new laws against dissenting sects, and also pushed for Cary's arrest. Cary responded by rebelling against the northern government, centered in Bath, where Cary lived. His followers were mostly among the dissenters and the residents of Bath County; the Quakers provided various means of support, although due to their pacifism, they would not have participated in the violent parts of the insurrection. When Hyde was unable to come to any terms with Cary, he in turn gathered a force of 150 men and attacked Cary's men but was repulsed. Other engagements followed, with inconclusive results. In July, Gov. Alexander Spotswood of Virginia decided to intervene on Hyde's behalf, sending militia and a force of Royal Marines. Cary fled to Virginia but was captured and with his chief supporters sent to England to stand trial before the Proprietors themselves. For whatever reason, no one appeared at the trial to press charges, so Cary was released, returned to Bath County, and lived quietly until his death a few years later. The conflict continued to reverberate in Carolina, however, and weakened authority at the province just prior to the eruption of a series of major wars with the Indians.

September 10, 1711–February 11, 1715

The Tuscarora War erupted in September 1711 at a time when Carolina was in a weakened state due to the conflicts between the Cary and Hyde factions in the Albemarle region and the Gibbes and Broughton factions in Charles Town. The Tuscarora are an Iroquoian Indian tribe. The expansion of Whites into Tuscarora lands, along with the kidnapping and enslavement of Tuscarora by Whites, led to tensions which erupted into warfare when Chief Hancock of the Lower Tuscarora, allied with various Algonquian Indian tribes, began to attack settlers near Bath and along the Roanoke, Neuse, and Trent Rivers. Hundreds of settlers were killed and others captured. Hyde asked for help from South Carolina, and Col. John Barnwell led a group of fifty White officers and 500 Indians who arrived in North Carolina in January 1712. Joined by a small party of North Carolina militia, Barnwell's expedition drove the Tuscarora back, leading to a truce and the release of prisoners. The South Carolinians then departed, however, unhappy over not being paid for their assistance, while North Carolinians were angry that the expedition had not pressed for a total defeat of the Tuscarora. The South Carolinians took with them some Tuscarora as slaves, leading to a new series of Indian attacks at a time when a yellow fever outbreak hit the colony, claiming Hyde as one of its victims in September 1712. His replacement, acting Gov. Thomas Pollock, requested help from South Carolina in turn. Col. James Moore led a new expedition of thirty-three Whites and a thousand Indians in December 1712.

In conjunction with Moore's expedition, the Whites decided to play different factions of the Tuscarora against each other. Although Hancock's Lower Tuscarora were fully engaged in the conflict, the Upper Tuscarora of Chief Tom Blount were not. The colonists offered support for Blount as chief of the entire Tuscarora tribe in exchange for his help in defeating Hancock's faction. Blount allied with the settlers. Hancock was defeated, captured, turned over to the colonists, and executed, and the Lower Tuscarora were decimated. Many were killed, or captured and enslaved, while others scattered throughout North Carolina. A few hundred left North Carolina, went northward, and became the Sixth Nation of the Iroquois Confederation. Blount assumed leadership of all the remaining Tuscarora in the state, but over time their numbers declined and their erstwhile colonial allies began to encroach on their territory again. The power of the eastern tribes in North Carolina was permanently broken by the war.

January 24, 1712

The partition of Carolina into North Carolina and South Carolina went into effect on this date, with Edward Hyde becoming first governor of North Carolina. Charles Craven had been appointed governor of Carolina in February 1711 by the Proprietors but had not arrived at the time of the partition, leaving Robert Gibbes in his anomalous position of acting governor, even though his election had been disallowed by the Proprietors. Craven arrived and assumed office as governor of South Carolina on March 12, 1712.

April 14, 1715–late 1717

In the aftermath of the Tuscarora War, the Yamasee War broke out in South Carolina in April 1715. The Yamasee were allies of the colonists during the Tuscarora War and had participated in both the Barnwell and Moore expeditions from South Carolina to North Carolina against the Tuscarora. Facing their own pressures from settlers moving into the South Carolina backcountry, and angered over the often-dishonest practices of colonial traders, the Yamasee killed most of small party of men on the night of April 14–15 sent by the South Carolina government to secure Yamasee support in the midst of rumors that the Creek were planning to attack the settlers. One of the two men who escaped managed to warn settlers in the Port Royal area, and thus there was some preparation when the Yamasee struck Port Royal the next day. Another Yamasee war party attacked St. Bartholomew's Parish and killed many settlers. Over the next several months, other tribes joined the Yamasee, including the Creek, as well as several smaller tribes, many of which, like the Yamasee, had allied with the colonists in the Tuscarora War. The Cherokee were initially divided, with the Lower Cherokee in particular in favor of the conflict. By 1716, the South Carolina militia had won some clashes with the Indians, and the Yamasee withdrew into central Georgia. Other tribes continued to fight, however, while the Cherokee decided to side with South Carolina against the Creek. Peace was made with the majority of the tribes individually by 1717.

July 25, 1729

North Carolina became a royal colony when the Lords Proprietor sold the colony to King George II. The colony had never been profitable for the Proprietors, while the monarchy had been purchasing proprietary colonies for some time; South Carolina, for example, had been purchased from the Lords Proprietor in 1719. One proprietor, John Carteret, 2nd Earl of Granville, refused to sell his share, but agreed to stay out of the governing affairs of the colony. After years of negotiation with the crown, it was agreed that Granville's share would be converted into a sixty-five-mile tract of land adjacent to the Virginia border running the length of the colony; this tract became known as the Granville Grant.

March 1733

The Molasses Act passed the English Parliament. Introduced at the behest of the large sugar plantation owners of the British West Indies, the law imposed a six pence per gallon duty on molasses imported into Britain or her colonies from other countries. The tax was opposed by Britain's American colonists, and a system of smuggling arose to circumvent it.

March 13–May 20, 1741

The Siege of Cartagena de Indias, part of the War of Jenkins' Ear, in which approximately 400 North Carolinians participated, began in March 1741. Located in modern-day Colombia, Cartagena was a major port in the Viceroyalty of New Granada, the Spanish province that at the time incorporated most of northern South America. The siege was part of a broader plan by Britain to seize Spain's four major ports in the region, which besides Cartagena were Vera Cruz in modern day Mexico, Portobelo in modern-day Panama, and Havana in modern-day Cuba. The British captured Portobelo in 1739. In 1740, they dispatched a large fleet commanded by Admiral Edward Vernon to take the other ports. Vernon decided that his first target would be Cartagena. Of the 12,000 soldiers that participated in the operation under the command of British Lt. Gen. Thomas Wentworth, the North Carolinians were part of a 3,600-man colonial force whose other men were recruited from Virginia, Pennsylvania, New York, Massachusetts, Rhode Island, Connecticut, New Jersey, and Maryland. It was organized into a regiment of four battalions commanded by Virginia's lieutenant governor, Col. William Gooch, and was known as Gooch's American Regiment. The regiment quickly gained a bad reputation for its lack of discipline. The Americans participated in an attack on Fort San Lazaro, which dominated Cartagena's land defenses. The attack took place before dawn on April 20, and the members of Gooch's American Regiment were charged with carrying the ladders for the assault as well as packs of wool to fill in the trench outside of the fort's walls. When the Spanish defenders opened fire on the attackers, most of Gooch's men dropped their ladders and packs and took cover. Their behavior was singled out for scornful criticism in the official reports of the campaign. Yet the problems of the expedition lay much deeper than the behavior of the colonial troops, as the lack of cooperation between Vernon and Wentworth and their poor individual decisions doomed the expedition. Furthermore, the attackers were decimated by the outbreak of disease, particularly yellow fever, that killed many and weakened most of those left. The British abandoned the expedition in May and sailed to Jamaica, and the Spanish soon recaptured Portobelo. Vernon and Wentworth invaded Cuba on August 4, but after four months of little progress withdrew on December 5. Additional actions in the Caribbean were also unsuccessful, and in September 1742, both Vernon and Wentworth were recalled in disgrace. The British and colonial losses in the Caribbean operations were high, with ninety percent losses to both combat and, in particular, disease among the troops; in some accounts Gooch's Regiment had only around 300 survivors.

September 4–6, 1748

Two Spanish privateers raided Brunswick Town in North Carolina as part of the War of Jenkins' Ear/War of the Austrian Succession. In fact, the two interrelated conflicts were over, as the Treaty of Aix-la-Chapelle had been signed on April 30. However, word of the peace treaty had not reached all parts of the globe by September. The Spanish ships, as well as a third vessel, a recently captured British ship, arrived off Brunswick Town on September 4 and anchored. While the inhabitants hid in nearby woods, the raiders plundered the town. Capt. William Dry III rallied a small band of the townspeople who surprised and attacked the Spanish on September 6. They soon withdrew to their ships, having lost forty casualties, including ten killed. During the fighting, one of the Spanish ships was hit by a small cannon crewed by Dry's men and exploded. Meanwhile, the British captives on the captured vessel overpowered the Spanish and ran the ship aground. The second Spanish ship agreed to surrender, as long as they would be allowed to depart. A sizeable band of colonial reinforcements arrived from Wilmington after the fighting had ended. The remaining Spanish ship slipped away overnight, taking with it some captives who they had promised to exchange for some of their own men captured in the fighting. As a result of this, the angry colonists sold the Spanish captives into slavery.

June 10, 1751

The Currency Act of 1751 restricted the issuance of paper money (or bills of credit) and the establishment of new public banks by the New England colonies, which had used them to pay for military expenses during the colonial conflicts. This paper money was not backed by specie, and because more of it was issued than taxed out of circulation, inflation skyrocketed. British merchants in particular were hard hit when bills of credit were used to pay private debts by citizens. The Currency Act allowed for the continuation of the use of already circulating bills of credit to be used for public debt, such as taxes, but not for private debt, such as paying merchants.

June 19–July 11, 1754

The Albany Congress met in Albany, New York. It was the first meeting of representatives from various colonies to discuss common issues, and a model for later ones to come. The colonies that sent representatives were Connecticut, Maryland, Massachusetts, New Hampshire, New York, Pennsylvania, and Rhode Island; New Jersey and Virginia were invited to participate but did not send representatives. The congress did not represent an independence movement, and in fact, met at the request of the British Board of Trade. Instead, its delegates sought to devise a treaty with the six Iroquois tribes and to plan common defensive measures against the forces of the French, based in what is now Canada. At the Congress, Benjamin Franklin introduced a plan for a unified colonial government under the British crown. It was intended to include all the British mainland colonies except for Delaware and Georgia, including those that did not send representatives, and would have led to the creation of a Grand Council made up of members selected by the colonial legislatures and presided over by a President General selected by the British government. The colonial assemblies voted against accepting the plan, however, protective of their colonial charters, jealous of their own prerogatives, and fearful of a centralized taxing authority. Likewise, the Board of Trade vetoed the plan, and never passed it along to the monarchy and Parliament for approval.

1758–1761

The Anglo-Cherokee War, partially connected to the French and Indian/Seven Years' War, was fought. Originally the Cherokee were allies of Britain and the colonists, but French representatives to the Overhill Cherokee in what is now Tennessee were successful in winning some chiefs to the French side, and the French planned to build forts in Cherokee territory in Mississippi and Alabama (but not in North Carolina). There were also plans for a native alliance consisting of the Cherokee, Shawnee, Muscogee, Catawba, and Chickasaw peoples, although it did not reach fruition. The British, in turn, built some forts within Cherokee territory. The conflict had multiple sources but can be boiled down to British mistrust of Cherokee motives, leading to a surprise attack against the Cherokee by members of the Virginia Militia as "reprisals" for the supposed theft of horses. The violence was the result of a misunderstanding about when and how the Cherokee would be compensated for their assistance. The Cherokee launching retaliatory raids into Virginia and the Carolinas. Cherokee leadership was divided, as some chiefs urged against a conflict. In North Carolina, the war included raids in early 1760 and an attack on Fort Dobbs in Rowan (modern Iredell) County on February 27. A British expeditionary force marched north from South Carolina under Col. Archibald Montgomerie in 1760 and successfully destroyed several Cherokee villages as it advanced into North Carolina. On June 27, Montgomerie's column encountered the Cherokee in the Battle of Echoee (Etchoe Pass) in modern-day Macon County. The clash halted Montgomerie's drive, due to the number of his casualties and the loss of many of his pack animals. In 1761, a second expedition was launched from South Carolina under the command of Maj. James Grant. It not only included British regulars, but such future South Carolina Revolutionary War luminaries as Francis Marion, William Moultrie, and Charles Cotesworth Pinckney. The new expedition also marched north and destroyed several villages. On June 10, the British and colonials clashed with the Cherokee near the site of the previous year's fight in Etchoe Pass. After several hours, the Cherokee were forced to withdraw as they ran out of ammunition. Grant followed up the clash with a brutal campaign, destroying several villages and killing many Cherokee or rendering them homeless. By July, the Anglo-Colonial column had exhausted itself and turned back, but the damage to the Cherokee heartland had already been done. The Cherokee agreed to separate peace treaties with Virginia and South Carolina in 1761.

January 25–29, 1759

The first of the so-called "Enfield Riots." The riots marked the culmination of unrest in the colonial counties of Granville, Halifax, and Edgecombe involving the Granville Grant, the last of the original Carolina proprietary tracts. The area was long known for its corrupt administration, especially in relation to land ownership, most of which was directly owned by the Granville family in England. On the night of January 25, residents of Halifax and Edgecombe Counties seized Francis Corbin and Thomas Bodley, land agents for Lord Granville, in Edenton. Corbin and Bodley were jailed for four days until they agreed to allow public inspection of land records. Corbin was also forced to post bond to appear at the superior court spring term, and to refund money taken illegally by his agents.

Granville subsequently suspended Corbin and Bodley. While many of the rioters are unknown, those who have been identified were members of the area's elite, rather than the poor. They were acting illegally, however, and some were subsequently arrested and jailed. Along with the later "Sugar Creek War," the Enfield Riots were early examples of backcountry unrest which would soon spawn the Regulator movement.

May 14, 1759

The second "Enfield Riot." A mob attacked the jail holding the arrested abductors of Corbin and Bodley and set them free.

October 25, 1760

George III, grandson of George II, became king of Great Britain.

1761

Henry McCulloh (ca. 1700–1779), a British governmental clerk and landholder and former provincial official in North Carolina, gave to the Earl of Bute his essay "Miscellaneous Representations Relative to Our Concerns in America." It argued for establishing a western boundary line in order to better manage relations with the Native peoples, and in order to increase revenue, lowering duties on imported rum and molasses into the colonies and collecting them more efficiently. It also argued that duties should be imposed on the stamped paper required for many official documents and that colonial currency should be standardized. McCulloh's ideas would become official British policy and spark the opening conflicts between the colonies and Britain. It is not known, however, how much McCulloh's essay exercised any influence on their actual adoption, especially as they were not introduced as parliamentary acts until fiscal necessity caused the government to cast about for solutions. Given that they were presented to Bute, however, it is very possible that McCulloh's ideas were filed away for future reference and that Bute may have shared them with allied political figures.

May 1762

John Stuart, 3rd Earl of Bute, became prime minister of Britain. Bute had been King George III's tutor beginning in 1751. Ambitious for power, he maneuvered his way between 1760 and 1762 into becoming prime minister, replacing the administration of Thomas Pelham-Holles, 1st Duke of Newcastle. This ended a long period of dominance of British

King George III in England, painted at the time of his coronation in 1760. The king believed in a more traditional, strong role for the monarchy, and often struggled with Parliament in his efforts to have his wishes enacted. He also faced conflict with his colonial subjects in North America, who wished a larger role of self-determination within the framework of the British Empire. This conflict eventually led to rebellion and a shift toward independence, something the king stubbornly resisted as he attempted to subdue the colonies, no matter the cost. Allan Ramsay, King George III in Coronation Robes , c. 1765, oil on canvas, 92.99 x 62.48 in., accessed Feb. 13, 2026, https://en.wikipedia.org/wiki/George_III#/media/File:Allan_Ramsay_-_King_George_III_in_coronation_robes_-_Google_Art_Project.jpg government by the Whig faction, supporters of a constitutional monarchy and a parliamentary system. Bute was a member of the rival Tory faction, which supported a strong and dominant monarchy.

September 1762

As the Seven Years' War wound down, George III wrote Bute about maintaining the army as close to its present size as possible, but at a cheaper expense than before 1749.

Many military officers were members of Parliament and beneficiaries of royal patronage, and in turn gave the king and the ministries political support. Over the next few months, the king struggled to come up with a postwar military budget and began to think of the role the colonies might play in paying for the army. Bute and other officials, meanwhile, also saw a role for the expanded postwar army, particularly in protecting the colonists from the Native Americans and from France and Spain, and in enforcing regulation of trade between the colonists and the Natives to prevent colonists from encroaching on Native lands, a major source of friction.

February 10, 1763

The Treaty of Paris ended the French and Indian War/Seven Years' War. The war caused Great Britain to assume massive amounts of debt. The need to repay those debts led to the various tax and revenue acts passed by Parliament that affected both the citizens of Great Britain and Britain's colonists abroad in the years following the war.

Part III

The American Revolution: From Political Protest to the Declaration of Independence, 1763–1776

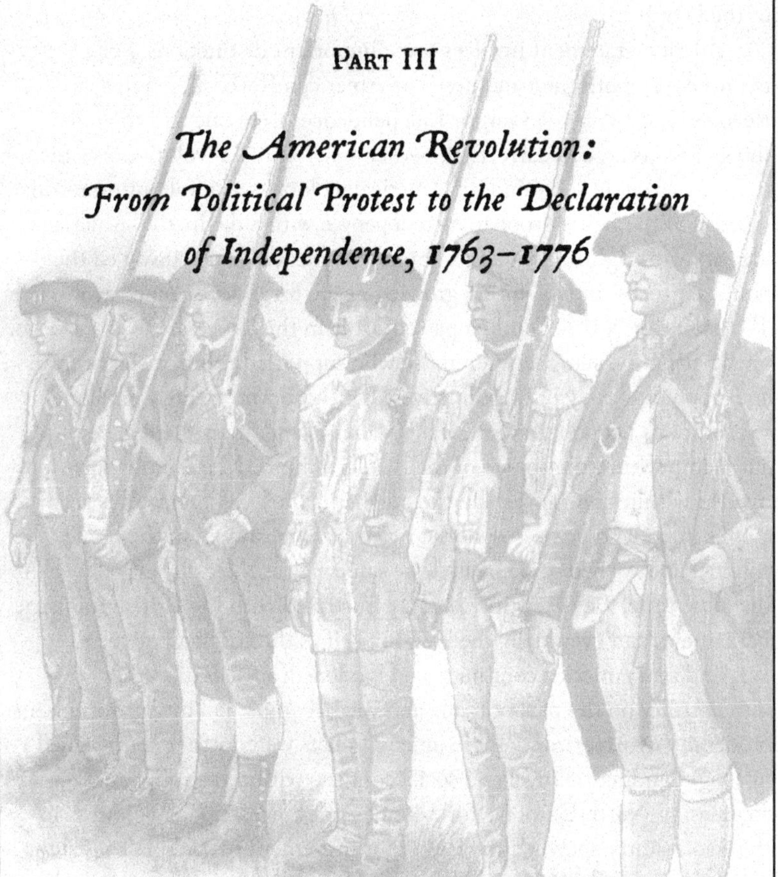

In an 1818 letter to publisher Hezekiah Niles, former revolutionary and U.S. president John Adams discussed the nature of the American Revolution. "But what do We mean by the American Revolution?," he wrote. "Do We mean the American War? The Revolution was effected before the War commenced. The Revolution was in the Minds and Heart of the People."

Adams's statement involves some important distinctions. For many people, both then and now, the American Revolution and the Revolutionary War (or War for Independence) were one and the same thing. Adams argued correctly, however, that the real revolution was the transformation in the minds of American colonists as loyal but protesting subjects of the British monarchy to a people with a distinctive American identity with rights and a desire for independence. It also involved the political process in which that growing desire for independence evolved. The people of North Carolina played a role in this process. Divisions developed within the state between those who supported the British government and labored to carry out its directives, and those who wanted Parliament to modify its tax policies toward the colonists and grant them greater autonomy within the sphere of the British Empire. Many individuals felt divided within themselves. On the one hand, they saw themselves as loyal Englishmen who possessed all the rights of Englishmen in the home country, and wished to be treated the same way as their distant fellows. At the same time, they grew increasingly frustrated with the British ministry, Parliament, and eventually the king himself as the conflict between England and America continued and hardened, a frustration that grew into hostility on the part of many and was accompanied by a growing sense of identity as Americans. These inner conflicts were further complicated by long-standing political and social conflicts within the individual colonies. In North Carolina, for example, grievances among colonists in the backcountry spawned the Regulator movement which challenged the colony's eastern political establishment. There is not a straight line running between this conflict and the Revolution as many of those who supported the Regulator movement would remain loyal to the Crown, while many of the members of the colonial government who suppressed the Regulators embraced the Patriot cause. Nevertheless it was still part of the backdrop of the Revolution's era of political and social unrest, sharing with it a struggle for individual rights against the excessive powers of unchecked government.

Once the fighting broke out in 1775, most of the initial conflict was in the Northern and mid-Atlantic colonies. This was partly due to the fact that the opening shots occurred in Massachusetts, center of so much of the leading Revolutionary unrest to that point. Britain initially attempted to hold onto Boston, but was quickly besieged by colonial militia following Lexington and Concord. The leaders of the Patriots or Whigs, the militant colonial movement, attempted on the one hand to achieve some sort of reconciliation with Britain, while at the same time creating some of the aspects of an independent national government, including a unitary colonial governing body in the Continental Congress along with an army and navy. The colonists also attempted aggressive military actions on their own, including an attempt to conquer the northern province of Quebec (modern Canada) which failed miserably.

While much of the major early military actions were in the North, the Southern colonies were not free of conflict. Much of it was internal, as the Royal governors attempted to hold on to power against an increasingly well-organized and powerful opposition. Despite the Crown still having many friends in the South, the Patriots soon gained the initiative, with the Southern governors having to take refuge offshore in British warships while the Patriots organized their own provincial governments. In the meantime, the beleaguered governors attempted various efforts to rouse and organize support among the Loyalist members in their populations. One particular measure caused controversy even among their own supporters, which were the attempts by some to arouse enslaved persons to desert their masters and perhaps to even enlist in exchange for freedom.

In North Carolina, Royal Gov. Josiah Martin attempted to unsuccessfully squash the Patriot movement following the outbreak of fighting but failed. The Patriots established their own provincial government and quickly began to suppress Loyalists in North Carolina. Rumors swirled around that Martin intended to rouse the enslaved to revolt and enlist the Cherokee to ravage the frontier. And indeed, the colonists soon found themselves in conflict with the Cherokee, although this had more to do with Indian reactions to continuing settler expansion into their territory than the machinations of Martin or Britain's Indian agents in the South. Martin, however, successfully roused Loyalists to organize against the rebels. The call for action was part of a plan in which the Loyalists would march to the coast, where they would be met by British ships and troops. With a contingent of British regulars operating with the Loyalists, chances for a royal recovery of the colony were high. Unfortunately for the Loyalists, they not only acted prematurely, before they were fully organized, but bad weather delayed the arrival of the British, and the Loyalists were defeated by Patriot forces at Moore's Creek Bridge.

Although the plan failed, it and subsequent British operations against Charleston, South Carolina, laid the foundations for the "Southern Strategy" of British political and military leaders that would lead to the climax of the fighting in North America.

This section will cover the evolution of the Patriot movement from one of loyal protest of the new taxation laws in the years following the conclusion of the Seven Years' War to the Declaration of Independence, including the outbreak of the war. The remainder of the military conflict will be covered in the following section.

April 8, 1763

An increasingly unpopular Lord Bute resigned the office of prime minister. Nevertheless, during the years leading up to the American Revolution, it was erroneously believed by many American colonists that he still held influence over George III and was in some way responsible for the taxation and other policies that increasingly angered them; for this reason, he often was mentioned as a figure of invective in anti-British colonial rhetoric. He was succeeded in office by a member of the rival Whig faction, George Grenville (1712–1770), who also became Chancellor of the Exchequer. Although a Whig, Grenville's personal ambitions had led to his estrangement from many of his Whig colleagues, and he was a member of Bute's administration and his personal choice to succeed him. It was Grenville who set the framework for monetary reform that included the earliest of the measures leading to conflict between Britain and the colonies.

May 9, 1763–July 25, 1766

Pontiac's War involved attacks by several American Indian tribes on British-occupied forts in the northwest, and the subsequent British retaliations. The conflict reinforced among the British authorities the sense that Indigenous American lands needed to be protected from encroachment by would-be settlers, which would reduce retaliatory attacks and prevent war.

September 1763

Lt. Gen. Thomas Gage was appointed commander-in-chief of British North America.

October 7, 1763

The British government introduced the Proclamation Line, separating settled lands and lands which could still be settled from the domains of American Indian tribes. The line ran along the Appalachian Mountains, cutting off many areas already settled by colonists. The measure sparked resistance as many colonists violated it and continued to explore and settle beyond the line.

April 5, 1764

Parliament passed the Sugar Act (the American Revenue Act/American Duties Act), the first in the series of major postwar acts that increased tensions between the British government and colonial Americans. The Molasses Act of 1733 had never been efficiently collected. It was thought that if the rate of the duty were reduced, theoretically making it less onerous, and if the lower amount was collected diligently, then the lesser amount imposed would bring in more revenue than had previously been the case. The Grenville administration introduced legislation which halved the old Molasses Act rate from six to three pence and also added new products to the list of enumerated items that the colonists could export only to Britain, most importantly lumber. Various means were provided for enforcing the act. Grenville hardly expected for the colonies to assume the burden of paying off the massive imperial war debt, but he did expect Americans to at least pay for their own defense and believed that the Sugar Act would provide much of the revenue to do just that. Unfortunately for Grenville and his colleagues, an efficiently collected tax was the last thing that Americans wanted, and smuggling had increased during the chaos of the conflict. In addition, the enforcement measures in the new act, including detailed ship manifests that had to be verified before the vessels could be unloaded in port, were time-consuming and annoying. Perhaps most troubling for many Americans was the shift of trial venue for those arrested on violation of the acts from local courts to far-away vice admiralty courts, which would be more ruthlessly enforced, and marked an intrusion of the military into civilian affairs. The latter provision convinced many colonists that something more sinister was afoot than an onerous new law. Gradually, a series of conspiracy theories were woven in which the British government sought to deprive the colonists of their liberties, although no such program was ever in place. An issue of contention began to emerge, however, over a more practical question: did Parliament have the right to impose external taxes on the colonies when the colonies sent no representatives to Parliament?

The members of the legislative body, as well as the imperial administrative system, all assumed that that answer was "yes," as it passed legislation on behalf of the empire. While colonial critics recognized Parliament's general authority, they increasingly argued that it did not have the right to impose taxes without representation and that revenue should be raised through the acts of the colonial assemblies. This reflected matters in Britain, where traditionally taxes were imposed only with the consent of the citizenry through their representatives. Supporters of the new law, and of Parliament's authority to impose taxes, argued that they colonists were "virtually represented" in Parliament by the collective members of the body themselves, as after all there were some who sat in Parliament who represented districts and communities that no longer had many inhabitants, while newer cities and towns had no direct representatives at all. Opponents regarded this as nonsense.

October 31, 1764

The North Carolina House of Commons denounced the Sugar Act to Gov. Arthur Dobbs.

March 1765

The "Sugar Creek War" broke out. An armed mob in Mecklenburg County attacked a surveying party working on behalf of Henry McCulloh, who had acquired large tracts of land in the southwestern region of North Carolina. At issue was McCulloh's insistence that he be paid for land sales in pounds sterling, while the residents wished to pay in provincial money. The mob broke the surveyors' equipment and chased off McCulloh's son, Henry Eustace McCulloh.

March 25, 1765

Parliament passed the Duties in American Colonies Act of 1765, better known as the Stamp Act. It provided for the collection of duties on the printed materials produced in London and bearing a revenue stamp that was required in the British realm for most legal documents, as well as playing cards and newspapers. The crucial difference between the Stamp Act and the Sugar Act, in terms of their respective impacts, was that the Sugar Act had its most important effects on ports and on those whose businesses dealt directly with molasses-related products, while the Stamp Act had the potential to affect everyone in the colonies.

March 28, 1765

Governor Dobbs died.

April 1765

A formal complaint was lodged with the Council of State over conditions in Mecklenburg County and the policies of McCulloh.

April 3, 1765

Lt. Gov. William Tryon became acting governor of North Carolina.

May 7, 1765

In the Sugar Creek district of Mecklenburg County, a second and more serious confrontation occurred between the locals and McCulloh's surveyors, when a group of men disguised with blackened faces beat the surveyors.

May 15, 1765

George III gave his assent to the Mutiny Act of 1765, North America, also known as the First Quartering Act. The law extended the British Army's right to quarter troops in certain designated buildings, both in Britain as well as the colonies. Troops would be quartered in military barracks and in public houses (pubs). If the number of troops exceeded available housing, then they would be quartered in inns, stables, taverns, uninhabited homes, outhouses, barns, and similar buildings. They were not to be quartered in private homes. The colonial governments would pay for these accommodations and the feeding of the troops. Although there would be invective, much of it inaccurate, directed at the British government over this law, it initially only had an impact in New York when the assembly refused to provide accommodations, resulting in the suspension of the governorship and the assembly by Parliament in 1767.

May 18, 1765

Lieutenant Governor Tryon prorogued the General Assembly until November 27. A term not widely known today, "prorogue" meant to discontinue a legislative session without outright dissolving it. Tryon was exasperated that the legislature accomplished little after sitting for two weeks, so he prorogued it with the hopes that, when it resumed, it would act in a more efficient manner. As a result, the General Assembly was not in session in June when the Massachusetts colonial assembly sent a letter to the other colonial assemblies suggesting a meeting for concerted action against the Stamp Act. The subsequent Stamp Act Congress was held in New York City in October, and North Carolina was not represented since the assembly had not been in session to choose delegates.

July 10, 1765

George III appointed Tryon governor of North Carolina.

July 11, 1765

The Stamp Office in London appointed Dr. William Houston as the stamp distributor for North Carolina, meaning he oversaw Stamp Act legislation for the colony.

July 13, 1765

The unpopular Grenville was replaced as prime minister by Charles Watson-Wentworth, 2nd Marquess of Rockingham, who was also appointed First Lord of the Treasury and became Leader of the House of Lords. Rockingham led the political faction known as the Rockingham Whigs and was a longtime political foe of both Bute and Bute's ally Grenville.

Among the members of his cabinet was the former prime minister, the Duke of Newcastle, who held the rank of Lord Privy Seal; and future prime minister the Duke of Grafton, appointed Secretary of State for the Northern Department. This first of two Rockingham administrations found itself preoccupied with the American colonial problems. Rockingham supported colonial rights and worked to get the Stamp Act repealed, although he also held that Parliament had a right to impose taxes on the colonies.

August 1765

The Sons of Liberty organized in Boston and gradually spread to other colonies, including North Carolina. They were established in opposition to the Stamp Act.

October 7–25, 1765

The Stamp Act Congress met in New York, New York. Nine of the eighteen British mainland colonies sent delegates: New York, New Jersey,

Rhode Island, Pennsylvania, Connecticut, South Carolina, Delaware, Maryland, and Massachusetts. Representatives were selected by the participating colonial assemblies. Other colonies showed interest in participating but failed to send delegates due to interference from their royal governors. In the case of North Carolina, Governor Tryon had, as previously noted, already prorogued the legislature until November on completely unrelated matters.

October 19, 1765

A large anti-Stamp Act demonstration was held in Wilmington, estimated in the local press to consist of nearly 500 people: "[A] certain HONOURABLE GENTLEMAN," a supporter of the Stamp Act, was hung in effigy. Barrels of tar were used to create a large bonfire, and the figure was thrown into the fire. Following the burning of the effigy, the mob went to each house in town, coerced all of "the Gentlemen to the bonfire, and forced them to drink a toast to "LIBERTY, PROPERTY, AND NO STAMP-DUTY," wishing "Confusion to Lord B-te and all his Adherents, giving three Huzzas at the Conclusion of each Toast." The activities concluded at midnight when the crowd "dispersed, without doing any Mischief." [Quoted from *North-Carolina Gazette* (Wilmington), November 20, 1765].

October 31, 1765

A second large anti-Stamp Act demonstration in Wilmington occurred the night before the law went into effect. Once again, a large crowd gathered, this time carrying "an Effigy of LIBERTY" placed in a coffin and carried in a funeral-like procession, accompanied by a drum and the town bell sounding a dirge. As part of the pageant, "before they committed the Body to the Ground, they thought it advisable to feel its Pulse; and when finding some Remains of Life, they returned back to a Bonfire ready prepared, place the Effigy before it in a large Two-arm'd Chair, and concluded the Evening with great Rejoicings, on finding that LIBERTY had still an Existence in the Colonies." [Quoted from *North Carolina Gazette* (Wilmington), November 20, 1765]

November 1, 1765

The Stamp Act went into effect.

In the fall of 1765, large demonstrations erupted in Wilmington over the Stamp Act. Passed by Parliament in March, the act imposed a tax on printed material produced in London, which required a revenue stamp. The act affected everything from legal documents to newspapers and playing cards. Protests had sprung up in many of the colonies throughout the summer but only reached North Carolina in October. Pressure was exerted on Gov. William Tryon to oppose the act and on stamp enforcer William Houston to resign. The unrest spread to Brunswick Town in the winter. By the end of February, the protesters were victorious. In February, the unrest throughout the thirteen colonies led to Parliament repealing the Stamp Act but still asserting their right to tax the colonies. Illustration by Stephen Marchesi.

November 16, 1765

The Sons of Liberty and a supporting mob in Wilmington forced Dr. Houston to resign as stamp distributor. They then pressured the editor of the *North Carolina Gazette* to publish the newspaper without the stamps, in violation of the law.

November 18, 1765

Tryon hosted a dinner with some fifty Patriot leaders from Brunswick, New Hanover, and Bladen Counties at his house, called Castle Tryon (formerly Russellborough and Castle Dobbs) in Brunswick Town, to defuse the Stamp Act unrest. He assured his guests that he was willing to use all his influence, consistent with his duty to the king and to Britain, to promote the well-being of the colony and its inhabitants. He was critical, however, of the behavior of those inhabitants of other colonies who had insulted royal officers or vandalized their homes and property, or who had burnt the stamp paper when unloaded. He hoped that nothing similar might happen if the stamps arrived in North Carolina and warned of "the disagreeable Consequence which might attend them." He refused to enter into a discussion of Parliament's right to tax the colonies, "but hoped that none in this Province were desirous of destroying the Dependance on the Mother Country; and therefore strongly urged the Prudence of not opposing the Legislature of Great-Britain." Tryon noted that all of the money in the colony would hardly pay for a year of the Stamp Tax, and that he intended to represent the situation to Britain in a way that the guests could reasonably expect would bring "a favorable Indulgence and Exemption of this Colony, unless his Endeavours were frustrated by the Conduct of the People," regardless of whether or not the tax was repealed. Tryon pointed out that if the stamps were accepted by North Carolina, an advantage would entail from commerce conducted as usual, as opposed to the colonies which had refused and thus impaired their own trade. He also offered to pay for all duties connected to any stamp paper used for any of his own economic interests.

November 19, 1765

After time for discussion, the guests returned to Tryon's residence, bringing with them an address. In it, the guests thanked Tryon for his willingness to advance the interests of the province. However, they also gave careful consideration to the Stamp Act and its provisions, and concluded that "every View of this Act, confirms us in our Opinion, that it is destructive of those Liberties, which, as British Subjects, we have a right to enjoy in common with Great Britain." The addressees acknowledged that they owed all loyalty to George III, albeit "consistent with the Rights of a free People," but believed the Stamp Act deprived them of their privileges as British citizens, and "naturally suggests to us" that submission to the law "is opening a direct Inlet for Slavery, which all Mankind will endeavour to avoid." They rejected Tryon's request, on the grounds that they would not concede Parliament's right to tax the colonies; this meant even rejecting Tryon's offer to pay the tax on documents related to his own financial dealings, as any concession to even a portion of the law would be an admission of the law's validity. Nor would they cede the right to a trial by a jury of their peers, rather than a trial by an Admiralty Court, which had traditionally been used for maritime cases only. The Patriot leaders promised they would use all of their influence to prevent any injury or insult to royal officers, "but must confess, that the Office of Distributor of the Stamps, is so detested by the People in general, that we don't think either the Person or Property of such an Officer, could by any Means be secured from the Resentment of the Country." They concluded by asserting their desire to promote the prosperity and continued interconnections of the colonies with Great Britain, and that they would "chearfully contribute all in our Power, to render your Excellency's Administration happy, easy and honourable." [Quotes from *North-Carolina Gazette* (Wilmington), November 27, 1765].

November 29, 1765

An armed group, led by Hugh Waddell and John Ashe, among others, refused the landing of stamps in Brunswick from the British ship *Diligence*. While many blamed the mob for blocking the stamps, others claimed that the stamps could not legally arrive in the colony, as North Carolina's office of stamp collector was vacant. Regardless, as a result, commerce stagnated; and further, at least according to the version that armed men prevented the unloading, Tryon shut down court transactions in retaliation. This in turn led to a freeze on commercial transactions.

January 14, 1766

H.M.S. *Viper* seized two ships in the Cape Fear River, the *Dobbs* of Philadelphia and the *Patience* of St. Christopher, because they lacked their stamped papers.

February 18, 1766

Leaders of the opposition to the Stamp Act in the Cape Fear region met in Wilmington. An "Association" was created to block the act's execution, even if their own lives and resources were threatened. The Stamp Act was declared to be "subversive of the Liberties and Charters of North America." Signers included John Ashe, Cornelius Harnett, and Hugh Waddell.

February 19, 1766

An armed mob, numbering in the hundreds, marched from Wilmington to Brunswick Town. Their object was the freeing of the *Patience* and another vessel, the *Ruby*, taken following the initial seizure of the *Dobbs* and the *Patience*. Upon arrival, a contingent was detached to surround the governor's house. The remainder then moved on to the customs house and seized the papers of the two ships.

February 20, 1766

The crisis at Brunswick Town continued. By this date, the mob had grown to nearly a thousand men. Moving to the docks, they boarded the *Viper* and forced its captain, Jacob Lobb, to release the seized boats. Lobb formally recorded his intention to release the vessels without noting the circumstances under which he had been forced to do so. From this point on, ships were able to enter the Cape Fear River without stamps.

February 21, 1766

The Brunswick Town crisis concluded. On this day, the mob again surrounded the home of Gov. William Tryon and demanded the surrender of comptroller of customs William Pennington. The governor refused. A story that Pennington hid under Tryon's bed may be apocryphal. Cornelius Harnett met with Tryon and warned him that the mob would seize Pennington if he did not give himself up. Tryon and Pennington agreed. The latter was escorted by the mob to the central part of town, where he and other government officials took an oath not to execute the Stamp Act. Pennington also resigned. By coincidence, on the same day, Parliament voted 276–168 for a resolution which repealed the Stamp Act. It received George III's royal assent on March 18.

March 18, 1766

The American Colonies Act of 1766, recently passed by Parliament, was given George's royal assent, accompanied by the repeal of the Stamp Act and a revision of the Sugar Act (the Revenue Act of 1766) which reduced the amount of the molasses tax. Better known as the Declaratory Act, the American Colonies Act was in some ways an attempt to allow the repeal of the Stamp Act while at the same time saving face for Parliament, but it also laid the groundwork for future acts of Parliament concerning the colonies. It proclaimed Parliament's right to pass any laws or statutes necessary for administration or oversight of the colonies. No direct mention was made of taxation. The law thus brought a mixed reaction among the colonists who were elated over the repeal of the Stamp Act: some thought the direct omission of taxation was an admission that Parliament did not have a right to tax the colonists without their consent, while others recognized that the right to pass any legislation affecting the colonies could in fact include taxation. The measure thus did not arouse a strong united reaction among the colonists, as some felt that they were victorious against Parliament, while others were burdened with forebodings about what the future might bring.

July 30, 1766

His administration weakened by dissent within its ranks, Rockingham resigned as Prime Minister. He was replaced by the most celebrated politician in England, William Pitt, Earl of Chatham, who had been the prime minister during much of the Seven Years' War and whose policies played a crucial role in Britain's victory. He was now plagued by health problems, however, and gradually assumed a lesser role within his own administration.

August 1766

A broadside circulated during the Orange County court session at Hillsborough, denouncing abuses of power by officials and calling for a meeting between citizens and officials.

Later known as Regulator Advertisement No. 1, the publication of this document in many ways marked the beginning of the Regulator movement in the backcountry. The Regulators had numerous grievances:

• Extortion and general corruption on the part of officials, particularly in connection with land ownership. In Orange County, much of the local ire was directed at Edmund Fanning, a New York transplant and friend of Governor Tryon who served as Superior Court judge, county registrar, assemblyman, and militia colonel.

• An inequitable tax system, in which the public was overburdened by taxes and various fees associated with legal transactions. A source of particular resentment was the poll tax on all White males over the age of sixteen and all free and enslaved Blacks over the age of twelve, which hit the poorer farmers hard while barely attracting notice from the large planters.

• The method of tax collection, which included the county sheriff having the right to confiscate the property of those unable to pay their taxes and sell the property at auction to meet the debt.

While Tryon attempted to curb the abuses, he was limited in what he could accomplish, especially as he did not want to spur conflict with the many legislators and local county officials who stood in the way of genuine reform.

October 10, 1766

In response to the call for a meeting in Regulator Advertisement No. 1, a gathering was held at Maddock's Mill. Twelve representatives of the backcountry movement attended. The meeting was publicly denounced by Edmund Fanning.

March 1767

With the physical collapse of William Pitt, Chancellor of the Exchequer Charles Townshend gradually began to assume the dominant role in the Pitt administration.

June 5, 1767

The first of the so-called Townshend Acts, the New York Restraining Act of 1767, was passed by Parliament. Also known as the Suspending Act, it shut down the government of New York in retaliation for the colony's failure to comply with the 1765 Quartering Act. No bills could be passed by the legislature or signed by the governor until they complied with the act. The colony of New York acted on the principle that it could not be taxed by Parliament because the colony lacked Parliamentary representation. Realizing that it was it was in a fight that it could not win, the New York legislature reluctantly agreed to foot the bill for the support of some of the soldiers stationed in the colony. As a result, Parliament felt that compliance had been met and the law was never implemented.

June 26, 1767

The Revenue Act of 1767 was passed. The second of the Townshend Acts, it placed duties on a number of new items, including glass, lead, and paper. As in the case of the Sugar Act, there was a new enforcement clause against smuggling that caused many colonists consternation: the use of writs of assistance, or warrants that permitted searching for smuggled items on private property. Respect for private property was a hallmark of British constitutional rights, so once again many British Americans felt that they were being treated differently from their peers in the home country.

June 29, 1767

Parliament passed the third Townshend Act, the Indemnity Act of 1767. Concerned with the decline of the British East India Company due to the colonists' purchase of cheaper smuggled Dutch tea, the new law lowered tea duties to a rate below the smuggled average price of Dutch tea, hopefully encouraging the colonists to buy more British tea.

June 29, 1767

The fourth Townshend Act, the Commissioners of Customs Acts of 1767, was passed by Parliament. Up until this time, oversight of customs-related matters in the colonies had been overseen by the Customs Board in England, but this proved impractical. The new law created a Customs Board based in the colonies, specifically in the important port city of Boston, Massachusetts. The new board would be able to handle customs-related matters, including smuggling, more directly.

July 13, 1767

The Western Boundary Agreement of 1767. At the request of John Stuart, British Superintendent of Indian Affairs for the Southern Department, Gov. William Tryon sent a team to establish a firmer boundary line between North Carolina and the Cherokee. The commissioners, assisted by members of the Cherokee Nation, surveyed a fifty-three mile stretch of land beginning at the South Carolina border and then agreed that the remainder of the boundary would extend in a straight line to the Virginia border. The new boundary was proclaimed on this date, January 1, 1768, given as the point by which settlers beyond the line were to remove themselves. In addition, anyone desiring to trade with the Cherokee would have to apply for a permit from the governor before doing so.

September 4, 1767

Townshend died suddenly of a fever. Augustus Henry FitzRoy, 3rd Duke of Grafton and 1st Lord of the Treasury under Pitt, replaced Townshend as the dominant figure in the administration.

February 27, 1768

The Secretary of State for the Colonies, a new office, was established to handle colonial affairs, removing that function from the authority of the Secretary of the Southern Department. Wills Hill, Earl of Hillsborough, became the first holder of the office.

March–May 1768

In a series of meetings held in Orange County in March and April, supporters of the Regulator movement announced a refusal to pay taxes until confusion regarding conflicting tax rates given by Edmund Fanning and the county sheriff were resolved and all funds accounted for. Meanwhile, violence erupted in April, when the arrest of a Regulator and the seizure of his horse to pay taxes led to an armed party releasing him from the Hillsborough jail. They fired shots into Fanning's house for good measure. When the county militia was mustered, many announced their refusal to act against the Regulators. Fanning managed to secure warrants against many of the leaders but discovered that the Regulators planned to take the town, leading him to appeal to Tryon for assistance. Tryon agreed to call out the militia.

Meanwhile, a planned May 11 meeting between leaders of the Regulators and Orange County officials was preempted when Fanning arrested several of the leaders on May 2. When some 700 Regulators gathered in response, Fanning released two of the prisoners the following day. At the same time, Tryon's secretary Isaac Edwards visited the Regulator camp and assured the men that Tryon would hear their petitions if they would disperse. They complied.

April–August 1768

The Regulator movement spread beyond Orange County. The association's activities, including several acts of mob violence, were found in Anson, Rowan, Johnston and Cumberland Counties.

July 6, 1768

The final of the so-called Townshend Acts, the Vice Admiralty Court Act of 1768, was issued by the Lords Commissioners of his Majesty's Treasury more than a year after the other four acts and ten months after Townshend's death. For these reasons, some argue that it should not be viewed as one of the Townshend Acts, although it shares with them concerns over issues related to revenue collection and smuggling. The new measure created three new Vice Admiralty Courts to oversee customs-related cases, which would sit in Boston, Philadelphia, and Charleston. Trials would be conducted without a jury and by a judge only.

September 22, 1768

In Hillsborough, a major confrontation occurred between the Regulators and the colonial forces that fell just short of erupting into open fighting. Some 3,700 Regulators faced off against Governor Tryon and a 1,461-man strong militia contingent. Tryon demanded the surrender of five Regulator leaders and that the remainder must pay their taxes and disperse. If they did so, he would pardon everyone except for the leaders. Most of the Regulators left during the night. One Regulator leader, the Quaker Herman Husband, was acquitted of the charges against him, while three others were convicted but got off with short prison terms and fines.

Fanning was also put on trial and convicted of six charges of extortion, but his punishment was laughably small, only a penny and court costs. He was also forced to resign as county registrar.

October 14, 1768

Pitt resigned from the government due to poor health. Grafton became the new prime minister.

November 11, 1768

In the North Carolina General Assembly, Speaker of the House of Commons John Harvey of Perquimans County gave a speech denouncing the Townshend Acts as an infringement on North Carolinians' rights as British subjects, and strongly defended the view that the colonists could not legally be taxed without representation in Parliament.

May 16, 1769

The Virginia House of Burgesses passed the Virginia Resolves of 1769, which asserted that taxes in the colony could only be imposed by the governor and the legislature.

November 2, 1769

John Harvey introduced the Virginia Resolves to the North Carolina House of Commons. A committee of the whole house was formed, which issued a petition to the king accompanied by resolves modeled on Virginia's.

November 6–7, 1769

In response to the House of Commons' actions, Governor Tryon dissolved the assembly. Speaker Harvey in turn called for an illegal meeting of the House. The majority of the members participated. The legislators passed a set of resolves similar to the one formally passed in the House days earlier and joined other colonies in adopting a plan of nonimportation. Beginning January 1, 1770, enslaved persons, wine, and British-made goods would not be imported into the colony.

January 28, 1770

Grafton resigned as prime minister and was replaced by Frederick North, 2nd Earl of Guilford.

March 5, 1770

Most of the Townshend Acts were repealed, except for the one on tea, which Lord North insisted remain in order to assert Parliament's right to tax the colonies. The repeal bill was given royal assent on April 12. Coincidentally, the Boston Massacre occurred on the evening of March 5, as a result of ongoing tensions between the local populace and the British military garrison. The incident began when a mob confronted a sentry. An officer and seven soldiers were sent to the sentry's support. The troops were pelted with rocks, snowballs, and other debris. One of the soldiers, who had been knocked over, fired without orders when he picked up his musket, and the other soldiers soon followed suit with a stuttering, undisciplined series of shots—again without orders—killing three men, mortally wounding two, and injuring six others. Local Patriot leaders played up the incident as a wanton massacre committed by brutal British forces. In a subsequent trial, the British soldiers were represented by a legal team that included prominent Patriot leader John Adams. Six of the soldiers were acquitted, although two received manslaughter convictions on evidence that they had deliberately fired into the mob.

June 2, 1770

The Wilmington branch of the Sons of Liberty met and affirmed that the nonimportation policy would continue, despite the repeal of most of the Townshend Acts.

September 24–25, 1770

During the Orange County Superior Court session in Hillsborough, members of the Regulator movement staged a violent riot. Among other acts committed was the whipping of Edmund Fanning and the destruction of his home.

January 15, 1771

The Riot Act of 1771, also known as Johnston's Act, was ratified by the General Assembly. A measure intended to suppress the Regulator movement, the law gave the attorney general a full year to prosecute any accusations of rioting in any court that he chose. Those accused had sixty days to respond to a summons to appear in court, or would otherwise face being declared an outlaw who could be killed at will and whose property would be seized by the government. The Regulators responded by threatening defiance, while many ordinary citizens felt that the law infringed on their rights.

May 16, 1771

The Battle of Alamance brought the Regulator movement to a climax. Governor Tryon and a militia force of some 1,000 men confronted a Regulator force over twice their size at Great Alamance Creek. When Governor Tryon offered a truce, the Regulator force advanced to a position closer to the militia battle line. Fighting began about noon and lasted approximately two-and-a-half hours. In the end, the discipline and greater fire power capability of the militia prevailed over the larger number of Regulators, many of whom were unarmed. Tryon lost nine killed and sixty-one wounded; the Regulator casualties are unknown, but they were at least as heavy as those of the militia and may have numbered as high as 300. The battle broke the Regulator movement's momentum, although it did not end unrest in the backcountry or alleviate the grievances which

Josiah Martin, the last Royal governor of North Carolina. He was quickly forced to take refuge on a British warship after the outbreak of hostilities, effectively ending his governorship. That did not make him any less of an important figure, as his views on conditions in North Carolina and the rest of the South were a major influence on the development of British military strategy, in particular his claims that the majority of colonists were Loyalists only waiting arming and the support of British military forces to rise up on behalf of the of the King. State Archives of North Carolina.

produced it. Some have attempted to hail Alamance as the first battle of the Revolutionary War, years before Lexington and Concord; however, it is impossible to draw a straight line between the politics of the Regulator movement and the politics of either the later Whig/Patriot or Tory/Loyalist movements. The Revolutionary affiliations of many of the rank-and-file Regulators remain unknown, but among those who have been identified, while some indeed joined the Patriot cause, many others remained loyal to the British crown. Likewise, many of the militia officers who fought at Alamance later served as officers on the Patriot side; while the Regulators' nemesis, Fanning, followed Tryon to New York as his secretary. During the Revolution, he raised a regiment of Loyalists there.

June 30–July 1, 1771

Governor Tryon departed North Carolina to assume the post of Governor of New York. On the day following his departure, the Council of State met and selected James Hasell to serve as acting governor until a new governor was formally appointed by the British crown.

August 12, 1771

Josiah Martin (1737–1786) was appointed governor of North Carolina. A native of Dublin, Ireland, Martin was the son of a wealthy Caribbean planter and served as an officer in the British Army during the Seven Years' War.

June 9-10, 1772

H.M.S. *Gaspee*, a British naval vessel enforcing customs law in the waters off Rhode Island, ran aground in shallow waters in Narragansett Bay while chasing a suspected smuggler. At dawn, the ship was boarded by a group from Providence that rowed out to it, overcame its crew, and set it afire. No one was killed in the incident, although there were injuries. A royal commission established to investigate the incident was unable to positively identify any of the participants, who would have been transported to Britain for trial. This was the first significant act of violence by colonists against British authority in the lead up to Independence.

March 6, 1773

The North Carolina General Assembly passed a bill for the regulation and funding of the Superior Court system. It included a clause supporting the right of the courts to practice judicial seizure ("attachments") on property for the debt of foreigners who owned property in the colony. In the previous year, however, the British government determined that attachments could not be made on the property of those who were not actually residents of the colony in which they held property. For these reasons, Governor Martin was required to reject the bill. As the House of Commons refused to back down on the issue of attachments, the court system was in effect dead. This led Martin to create his own courts of oyer and terminer without legislative approval, considered by the legislature to be a major infringement on its power.

May 10, 1773

George III gave his assent to the Tea Act, a law passed by Parliament to aid the struggling East India Company. The company was allowed to export tea directly to the colonies, and duties normally applied in Britain prior to exportation were either refunded or ignored altogether.

These and other provisions would drastically lower the total price of tea, undercutting the price of the cheaper Dutch tea smuggled into the colonies. The reaction among the colonists was not as Britain hoped, however, as many objected to the fact that the tea tax from the old Townshend Acts was still on the books. Further, colonists opposed the law on the grounds that it gave a monopoly to the East India Company. The passage of the law opened the final series of crises that led to rupture between the colonies and Britain, beginning with the Boston Tea Party in December.

December 4–21, 1773

The General Assembly met and refused to fund Martin's courts of oyer and terminer. The House of Commons continued to refuse to budge on the issue of foreign attachments. With the lack of legislative action, Martin prorogued the legislature for three months on December 21. Meanwhile, in response to a letter from the Virginia Committee of Correspondence and Enquiry, the legislature formed its own standing committee in Wilmington, whose members were John Harvey, Robert Howe, Cornelius Harnett, William Hooper, Richard Caswell, Edward Vail, John Ashe, Joseph Hewes, and Samuel Johnston. As in the case of other colonies' Committees of Correspondence and Enquiry, the North Carolina branch gathered information about Parliamentary acts, disseminated the information to the public and to other committees, and corresponded with other colonies' committees about coordinated plans of resistance.

December 16, 1773

The Boston Tea Party occurred on this date. The reaction to the 1773 Tea Act in the colonies was largely negative. Ships carrying tea sailed for Boston, New York, Philadelphia, and Charleston. In all of these ports but Boston, those officially consigned to receive the tea were forced to resign by protestors organized by the Whig movement, and the ships turned back with the tea undelivered. In Boston, however, the consignees were fully backed by Gov. Thomas Hutchinson and did not resign. Crowds prevented the tea from being unloaded ashore. The price of the tax was not an issue, as the Tea Act lowered the amount of the tax on that product; instead, it was the ongoing opposition to Parliament having the authority to tax, considered to be an infringement on British American liberties. On the night of December 16, 1773, thousands gathered near the Old South Meeting House in Boston, where Whig leaders held a meeting over the controversy. By this time there were three British ships at anchor in the port's harbor. Matters were in deadlock, as the protesters still refused to let the tea be unloaded, but Hutchinson likewise would not permit the ships to return to Britain without being unloaded. In the midst of the meeting, a small crowd, exact numbers unknown, left and headed for the wharf where the tea would have been unloaded. Some of the men were dressed and made up as Mohawks to conceal their identities. They boarded the ships and threw all of the tea chests, numbering 342, into the harbor. The dumping of the tea caused almost universal condemnation among Britain's political establishment, including those that had colonial sympathies. In response to the tea's destruction, Parliament passed the Coercive Acts the following year. In the meantime, various other incidents of protest against the Tea Act occurred in other colonies.

March 2, 1774

The North Carolina General Assembly met and continued to refuse to give way on the subject of foreign attachments. However, the legislature and the governor agreed on funding an inferior court system and the governor's courts of oyer and terminer. The Superior Court system would not be fully restored until the establishment of a Revolutionary colonial government.

March 20–June 22, 1774

The Coercive Acts were passed by Parliament and given royal assent. Known in the colonies as the Intolerable Acts, the laws were a series of punitive measures primarily issued in response to the Boston Tea Party. Some of the measures were directed specifically at the colony of Massachusetts, while others affected the colonies as a whole. The laws consisted of:

- **The Trade Act of 1774 (also known as the Boston Port Act)**, which received George III's assent on March 20, 1774. Beginning on June 1, the Port of Boston was closed until restitutions were made to the royal treasury for lost customs duties and the East India Company for damages.

In addition, Boston would lose its status as the colony's capital, with the government moved to Salem, while Marblehead would become the new colonial port of entry. The act would be enforced by British warships and troops.

• **The Massachusetts Government Act**, also given royal assent on March 20. It revoked the charter of the Massachusetts colony and concentrated power in the hands of the royal government at the expense of the colonial assembly and the colonists. The members of the executive council would no longer be elected but appointed by the king. Other civil offices that up until that point in time had been elected were now chosen by the king. This law was viewed as a threat by the other colonies.

• **The Act for the Impartial Administration of Justice**, or **Administration of Justice Act**, went into effect on May 20. It gave royal governors the chance to move the trial venues of royal officials accused of committing crimes while attempting to suppress riots and civil unrest from Massachusetts to another colony, or even to Britain itself, if the governor felt that they would not receive a fair trial.

• **A new Quartering Act**, became law on June 2. It provided for army officers to requisition unoccupied structures for their troops, and if necessary assisted by the royal governor in acquiring them.

• **The Quebec Act**, given royal assent on June 22, was not intended as any sort of punitive measure by the British government, but was regarded as one of the Intolerable Acts by the strongly anti-Catholic majority of the British colonial population. It expanded the territory of Quebec Province, granted free practice of Catholicism, removed references to Protestantism from the oath of allegiance, and used French civil law as the basis for private law.

In response to the acts, several colonies issued calls for a gathering of representatives to coordinate action. It was eventually decided that this proposed meeting, later known as the First Continental Congress, would meet in Philadelphia, Pennsylvania. In April, Governor Martin's secretary revealed to John Harvey that the governor would not call the legislature into session until after any such assembly was over, so that the legislature could not choose any delegates to represent North Carolina. As Harvey circulated the information to like-minded colleagues over the succeeding weeks, there was an increasing sense that some sort of meeting needed to be called to address current events.

July 21, 1774

A public meeting held in Wilmington discussed the political situation between the colonies and Britain. The meeting was the result of the issuance of the Coercive/Intolerable Acts and Governor Martin's decision not to call the legislature into session to prevent the choosing of North Carolina delegates for the First Continental Congress. At the meeting, William Hooper, Cornelius Harnett, and other political leaders called for the holding of a "provincial congress" to discuss a response to the crisis. Over the next few weeks, meetings were held in several counties to choose delegates. Any such gathering was considered extralegal, as it was organized without the consent of the royal governor or of the colonial legislature.

August 13, 1774

Governor Martin issued a proclamation condemning the call for a provincial congress as an illegal act.

August 25–27, 1774

The First North Carolina Provincial Congress met in New Bern. The extralegal gathering consisted of elected representatives from thirty-five counties to represent North Carolina in the First Continental Congress. John Harvey was chosen to be president of the congress. The body elected three men (Richard Caswell, Joseph Hewes, and William Hooper) to the First Continental Congress. The Provincial Congress declared that after January 1, 1775, they would not import East India or British goods, and if the grievances which they had sent to the Crown were not addressed, they would not export any goods to Britain after October 1, 1775.

August 27, 1774

The Louisa Company, a land speculation company whose goal was to develop the lands west of the Appalachian Mountains in defiance of the Proclamation of 1763, was organized by former North Carolina Superior Court judge Richard Henderson and several other prominent associates. On January 6, 1775, the company reorganized as the Transylvania Company.

Late Summer and Fall 1774

Elements among the colonists opposed to Britain's policies began to prepare for possible armed conflict. In August, a Dutch company based in Amsterdam shipped a cargo of gunpowder to the colonies, and American vessels may have picked up another shipment of military supplies at the same port in October. Reports of such activity filtered to the British authorities, and on September 1, Thomas Gage sent troops to take munitions and weapons from a powder magazine located near Boston. Alerted to the British plan ahead of time, the reaction to the seizure of the military supplies set off the so-called "Powder Alarm," in which the local Massachusetts militia gathered in force near Boston, albeit too late to confront the British troops and prevent the removal of the supplies. Their reaction led Gage to concentrate his troops in the vicinity of the town and ask for reinforcements from Britain.

September 5–October 26, 1774

The First Continental Congress sat in Philadelphia, Pennsylvania. On October 20, the assembly enacted the Continental Association, which called for nonimportation of goods from Britain and nonconsumption of British goods beginning December 1. It also called for a repeal of the Intolerable Acts by September 10, 1775, which if not enacted, would lead to the nonexportation of American goods to Britain.

September 21, 1774

A meeting was held by leaders of the Patriot movement in Worcester, Massachusetts. Disturbed by weaknesses in the current state of the colonial militia and the slow response time to the recent British raid on the powder magazine, the meeting recommended that one-third of the militia be organized into companies of "minutemen," ready to answer a call to action at a minute's notice. The members of the meeting also instituted a system of alerts and organized express riders to carry news rapidly. Although the idea of the minutemen was primarily a New England phenomenon, other colonies adopted the concept to some extent, including North Carolina, which in 1775 organized six battalions of minutemen for six-months' service.

October 5–7, 1774

Although prohibited by the Coercive/Intolerable Acts from meeting, the Massachusetts Provincial Assembly met illegally in Concord on

October 5 and reorganized themselves two days later as the Massachusetts Provincial Congress, with John Hancock chosen to be its president. Among its important acts was the decision to make the recommendation of the Worcester meeting in September more official and authorize that one-fourth of the colony's militia be organized into minuteman companies. Other colonies established provincial congresses in the coming months.

October 18, 1774

Concerned by reports that colonial governments, or various individuals or organizations within the colonies, had begun to purchase military supplies, George III issued Orders in the Privy Council that forbade the export of arms, ammunition, or gunpowder into the thirteen colonies. The illegal colonial munitions trade with the Dutch, joined by Britain's old foe the French, continued unabated in secret.

October 25, 1774

By this date, fifty-one women from the vicinity of Edenton, North Carolina, signed a resolution in support of the British boycotts introduced at the First Provincial Congress in New Bern two months prior. According to legend, Penelope Barker orchestrated the public resolution. Whether Barker was the ringleader or not, the signed resolution eventually made itself to the British press, where it was published in the *Morning Chronicle and London Advertiser* of January 15, 1775. It became the subject of derogatory comment in the British press, accompanied by a satirical engraving by Philip Dawe. Subsequently dubbed the Edenton Tea Party, it is considered a landmark political event because it was organized by, and consisted of, women acting independently.

December 12–15, 1774

Rumors circulated in New England that the British planned to send troops to Fort William and Mary, guarding the approach to Portsmouth, New Hampshire, to seize the munitions stored there. Paul Revere was sent from Boston to Portsmouth by the local Patriots as an express rider, giving the alarm as he went. The New Hampshire Patriots quickly organized, and on December 14, stormed the fort, which was guarded by a six-man garrison of provincial troops. Shots were exchanged and a hand-to-hand struggle ensued before the outnumbered guards were overcome. The Patriots removed the gunpowder at the fort. On the next day, more

A London newspaper cartoon satirizing the so-called Edenton Tea Party. Although the cartoon used typical techniques of the day to grossly caricature the signers, the fact that a cartoon was even created in the first place demonstrates that the women of Edenton had gotten the attention of both the British government and public. The "Tea Party" demonstrated to all that women were active participants in the Patriot movement. Philip Dawe, A Society of Patriot Ladies, at Edenton, North Carolina, 1775, mezzotint, accessed 23 Feb. 2026, https://commons.wikimedia.org//wiki/File:Edenton-North-Carolina-women-Tea-boycott-1775.jpg

Patriot militia gathered from New Hampshire and from the portion of Massachusetts that is now the state of Maine. This fresh force stormed the fort that night, removing additional munitions and several cannon. The military supplies seized in these raids were later utilized by the Continental Army in the Siege of Boston. The British government labeled the incident an act of treason.

January 1775–1782

The Great Smallpox Epidemic of North America raged throughout the British colonial zone and beyond, affecting colonists and American Indians alike. Outbreaks of the disease, which only affected humans and could only be spread by human contact, had happened many times before in the Western world over the past few centuries. The disease initially caused flu-like symptoms that resulted in blindness or death if left untreated. The outbreak seems to have begun in Massachusetts as early as February 1774, although it only gradually spread elsewhere. Intercolonial travel brought it to other places, such as Philadelphia. By January 1775, however, it had taken serious root in Boston, which as a major port town offered possibilities to spread the disease abroad. Matters worsened when military action broke out between the colonists and the British in the spring, as the concentration of troops and the penned-up population of Boston quickly became targets. Inoculation efforts among the rival armies gradually brought the disease under control, but not before it affected several military operations, particularly the Patriot effort to capture Quebec Province (modern Canada) from the British in 1775. Other combatants, such as militiamen, did not receive such protection, and casualties from the disease were high among them, as it was among civilians, enslaved peoples and Black refugees with the British, and especially among the Native American population. North Carolina had already suffered from a major smallpox outbreak in 1738–1739 which killed thousands. During the Revolutionary conflict, outbreaks in North Carolina were often directly connected to the passage of military forces through particular areas. By 1782, the epidemic began to die down in the new United States and in neighboring Quebec and Spanish Mexico; however, although documentary evidence is scant, it seems to have continued to spread across the Great Plains and to the Pacific coast, devastating the Indigenous populations.

March 1775

By early 1775, the Caribbean Island of St. Eustatius, controlled by the Dutch East India Company, had become a major source of supplies for the rebellious colonists. The Dutch had officially been an ally of Great Britain since the Glorious Revolution of 1688, and the current stadtholder (ruler) of the Dutch Republic was related to George III and hostile toward the American revolutionaries. The Republic, however, was a trading nation, and Dutch merchants were anxious to keep a policy of neutrality in play so that they could profit by trading with both Britain and the colonists. The legality of the colonial trade became more complicated in March 1775, however, when the Dutch government announced that it was forbidding trade in weapons and munitions to the colonists, a decision made under pressure from the British. A covert illegal trade would continue.

March 17, 1775

Richard Henderson met with leaders of the Cherokee Nation near the site of present-day Elizabethton, Tennessee. Henderson negotiated the "sale" of a vast amount of territory from the Cherokee, comprised of the lands bounded by the Ohio, Kentucky, and Cumberland Rivers, and a portion of the Cumberland Gap, in exchange for trade goods valued at around 10,000 pounds. As in the case of many such so-called "purchases" of land by settlers from American Indians, given the very different values and understandings of what constituted ownership and exchange of land, it is doubtful that the Cherokee actually intended to permanently convey the land in question to Henderson, especially since the territory included lands associated with rival nation the Shawnee that the Cherokee had no claim to. Regardless, explorers and settlers sponsored by Henderson began moving into the area in subsequent years and exacerbated tensions with native peoples throughout the region.

Ca. March 23–April 5, 1775

Sometime during this period occurred the event subsequently referred to as the Wilmington Tea Party, in which local women publicly burned their tea. The sole account of the event comes from an undated letter by Scottish traveler Janet Schaw, who visited her brother, a planter in Wilmington, and other friends in the area beginning in February 1775. It is likely that Schaw was an eyewitness to the event, which is otherwise obscure.

April 3–8, 1775

The Second North Carolina Provincial Congress met in New Bern from April 3 to April 7. The General Assembly of North Carolina also met in New Bern beginning on April 4, and most of the same men were in both meetings. Legislative activities essentially took a back seat to the meeting of the congress. Representatives were selected for the Second Continental Congress, to meet in Philadelphia the following month, and they endorsed the activities of the committees of safety and created a North Carolina Council of Safety. As a result of these actions, Martin dissolved the assembly on April 8.

April 19, 1775

British soldiers marching from Boston to seize reputed caches of arms near Concord, Massachusetts, exchanged shots with militiamen at Lexington and then were turned back by additional militiamen at Concord Bridge. On their return march to Boston, they were fired upon repeatedly by militiamen concealed along the roadsides. Although casualties were light on both sides, the skirmishes marked the beginning of a new and ominous turn in colonial and British relations, and in later times was understood to have marked the beginning of the American Revolutionary War.

April 19, 1775–March 17, 1776

The Siege of Boston began on April 19, 1775, as Massachusetts militia units began to block the roads leading to and from the port city in the wake of Lexington and Concord. Over subsequent days, the militia dug in, as did their British counterparts, fortifying various defensive positions. During the succeeding months, the British engaged in various military operations designed to drive the Patriot forces from positions where they could bombard the town, while the Patriot forces in turn gradually became more organized, particularly after the creation of the Continental Army by Congress.

April 21–May 4, 1775

The "Virginia Gunpowder Incident," occurred, an action taken by Virginia's Gov. James Murray, 4th Earl of Dunmore, to protect colonial military supplies from seizure by Whigs. Following the "Powder Alarm" in Massachusetts in September 1774, William Legge, 2nd Earl of Dartmouth and Secretary of State for the Colonies, wrote the royal governors of the North American colonies to remove their military supplies to safe places.

In Virginia, sympathizers to the Whig cause organized and equipped militia companies during the early part of 1775. On April 21, Dunmore sent Lt. Henry Collins and a party of Royal Marines to remove the gunpowder stored at the powder magazine in Williamsburg, the Virginia capital. They loaded it on to the HMS *Magdalen*, a British warship anchored in the James River. The removal and transportation of the gunpowder was seen by pro-Whig colonists, and a mob was organized while militia units were called out. The mob backed down and dispersed at the urging of Whig leaders and after Dunmore told the Williamsburg city council that he had moved the gunpowder to a place of safety due to rumors of an imminent slave revolt. The next day, he assumed a very different stance. Facing another mob, and pressured by members of the House of Burgesses to return the gunpowder, Dunmore threatened to free the slaves and burn Williamsburg down if he was attacked. Word of Lexington and Concord arrived by April 28, adding to the tensions. The Hanover County militia, led by Col. Patrick Henry, the fiery Patriot lawyer and orator, marched on Williamsburg on May 2 in an effort to force Dunmore to pay for the powder out of Crown revenue money. Dunmore ordered all militia units to refrain from marching on Williamsburg on May 3, as Henry's company approached the town. The governor's family had already fled Williamsburg, eventually finding refuge on a British warship in the York River. On May 4, Henry received a £330 bill of exchange for the powder, which Dunmore kept. The immediate crisis was over, but it foreshadowed other conflicts between Southern royal governors and supporters of the Patriot cause over arms and munitions, as well as Dunmore's later proclamation to free slaves who would fight for the British.

May 10, 1775

The Second Continental Congress sat in Philadelphia. North Carolina was once again represented by Caswell, Hewes, and Hooper. This body remained in control of the nascent Patriot government nationally through 1776, and in July 1776 its members signed the Declaration of Independence.

May 10–11, 1775

A Patriot force commanded by Ethan Allen and Benedict Arnold captured Fort Ticonderoga on Lake Champlain from the British on the night of May 10, while a second force under Seth Warner seized nearby Crown Point on the following day. The capture of Ticonderoga provided cannon which would later be used by the Patriots at the Siege of Boston, while the fort later provided a staging ground for a Patriot expedition against Quebec Province.

May 15, 1775

John Harvey died following a fall off his horse.

May 20, 1775

According to a newspaper account published in 1819, on this date a meeting of militia officers in Mecklenburg County issued and signed the Mecklenburg Declaration of Independence, declaring independence from Britain. Most historians believe that the declaration as published in 1819 represented a sincere but garbled effort to reconstruct the text of the much less radical Mecklenburg Resolves, issued on May 31 but the text of which was unavailable at the printing of the 1819 article; however, it soon became enshrined in state lore and state pride as truth that at least a portion of the colony declared independence from Britain over a year before the Declaration of Independence. It subsequently became the source of the state's "First in Freedom" slogan, and its supposed date was used by the secessionists of 1861 as the date on which the state seceded from the United States and joined the Confederate States of America.

May 23, 1775

In New Bern, Abner Nash led a mob of Patriots to the governor's palace in protest of the dismounting of the cannon stationed there. Martin had dismounted them to prevent the New Bern Committee of Safety from taking them. Martin's excuse to Nash was that they were being repaired, but neither he nor the mob were satisfied, and they seized and carried off the remaining cannon.

May 31, 1775

The Mecklenburg Resolves were adopted by the Mecklenburg County Committee of Public Safety. The resolves "annulled and vacated" all laws that derived their authority from either the British crown or Parliament. Instead, the resolves argued that all legislative and executive power in the colonies was vested in the Continental Congress. Reconciliation with Britain was only possible if Parliament conceded that it had no authority to impose its will upon the American colonies. It was not a declaration of independence, as it still held open the possibility of reconciliation. A copy was sent to North Carolina's representatives at the Second Continental Congress, but they declined to make them public as they were considered to be too radical at that time. The original handwritten record of the committee was destroyed by a fire in 1800, and the text of the Resolves was lost until 1847, when a copy of a June 1775 South Carolina newspaper was unearthed that had published the text. It is believed by many historians that the "Mecklenburg Declaration of Independence," mentioned for the first time in an 1819 newspaper, represented an effort to reconstruct the text of the Resolves by someone who remembered the actual document as having been even more radical than it actually was. In reality it would have been strange for representatives of the county to declare independence on May 20, only to issue another document eleven days later that held out the possibility of reconciliation with Britain.

June 2, 1775

Governor Martin arrived at Fort Johnston, near Smithville (modern Southport) and took refuge there, making it his headquarters.

June 14, 1775

The Continental Army was created by the Second Continental Congress, incorporating colonial forces already raised for the Siege of Boston and the defense of New York City.

June 15, 1775

George Washington was appointed commander of the Continental Army by the Second Continental Congress.

June 17, 1775

The Battle of Bunker Hill (Breed's Hill), Massachusetts. Part of the siege of Boston. The first major battle of the war. British plans to take two key positions on the high ground overlooking the town, Dorchester Heights and Breed's Hill, the latter on the Charlestown peninsula, were leaked to the Patriot forces, who quickly fortified Breed's Hill and, just behind it, Bunker Hill. On June 17, British troops landed on the Charlestown peninsula after a naval bombardment that set Charlestown afire. After three assaults the British carried the Breed's Hill redoubt, forcing the Patriot forces to retreat across Bunker Hill and abandon their position there. The British lost over 1,000 casualties, while the colonials lost between 400 and 500. Although a British victory, the clash showed that the colonists could stand up against British regulars. It also had the counterproductive effect of angering the British leadership and populace, undermining final peace feelers from the Continental Congress and hardening British resolve toward what was increasingly seen as a rebellion.

June 20, 1775

On this date, the Liberty Point Resolves were issued by fifty-five pro-Whig residents of Cumberland County who had formed an "Association." Known as the Cumberland Association, a term sometimes used to refer to the resolves themselves, the document was written after the arrival of the news of Lexington and Concord reached the area. The resolves decried the actions of the British government and affirmed a right for the colonists to fight in their defense, until America and Great Britain reconciled "upon constitutional principles, an event we most ardently desire." Although sometimes referred to as a "declaration of independence," which it was not, the Liberty Point Resolves joined the more detailed Mecklenburg Resolves as an assertion of open defiance of British actions while falling short of a true call for independence.

July 5, 1775

The Second Continental Congress passed the Olive Branch Petition, signed on July 8 by representatives from all the mainland colonies except Georgia. Drafted by John Dickinson of Pennsylvania, it asked for George III to establish a settlement of all the grievances between Britain and the colonies, beginning with a repeal of the Intolerable Acts, on a basis that would prevent all future conflict. It was sent to Britain on the day of the signing, carried by Loyalist and Proprietor Richard Penn Jr. of Pennsylvania and by Virginia-born Arthur Lee, at that time a British barrister but a Patriot sympathizer who later served as an American diplomat.

July 5, 1775

Elbridge Gerry of the Massachusetts Provincial Congress ordered pistols and ammunition from Diego María de Gardoqui y Arriquíbar, a member of the powerful Spanish mercantile family the House of Gardoqui and a partner in the Bilbao-based company José Gardoqui and Sons. The resulting shipment was made in secret, as Spain was at peace with Britain; however, all munitions made and shipped from Spain required approval by the government, so the action was done with the tacit assent of the authorities. Gardoqui continued to secretly ship arms and munitions to the

Patriots, and eventually became the official financial representative of the Spanish government to the Continental government.

July 6, 1775

The Second Continental Congress passed the "Declaration of the Causes and Necessity of Taking up Arms," written by Thomas Jefferson of Virginia and then heavily revised by John Dickinson. The resolution listed the various grievances held by the colonies against Parliament since the end of the Seven Years' War, accusing the British legislature of repeatedly violating the British Constitution and the rights of the colonists as British subjects. In a bit of unintended irony, slaveholder Jefferson likened the situation of the colonies to enslavement by Parliament.

The document strongly affirmed that the colonists were not attempting to rebel or seek independence from Britain but instead had decided to fight only to secure the colonists' rights.

July 6, 1775

The British Admiralty issued an order for the Royal Navy to seize and detain American vessels by establishing squadrons to patrol the areas off of New York, Delaware and Chesapeake Bays, and Charleston, thus marking the beginning of a partial blockade.

July 8, 1775

Responding to news that a slave rebellion was to be launched in Beaufort County that night, one hundred men of the Pitt County militia were ordered out by the county's Safety Committee. By the end of the day, forty alleged participants had been rounded up and jailed.

The revolt was said to have been organized by a Black man named Merrick, who at that time was owned by a Capt. Nathan Blinn of Bath Town, and a Capt. Johnson of "White Haven" (probably Whitehaven, England), whose vessel was anchored at Beaufort to take on naval stores. On the following day, the committee began to examine the accused, and details of the plot emerged, which involved the killing of all Whites in the province. Five of the Black captives were whipped on the committee's orders. On Monday, July 10, "several" of the captives were "severely whipt" and had their ears cropped publicly as punishment. That evening, fresh rumors came of armed Blacks operating along the Pitt and Chatham County borders, with a request for assistance. This was soon amplified to involve as many as 250 armed Blacks who had been subject to pursuit for some days prior, "but none taken nor seen tho' they were several times fired at." On July 11, the Pitt Safety Committee dispatched two cavalry companies to different points to investigate the accounts, but concluded that the rumor had been started by an enslaved woman who was conspiring to kill her owners and then place the blame on the band. She was given "severe correction." The committee continued to "keep taking up, examining and scourging, more or less every day" more suspects, who all confessed to similar stories of a plot involving an insurrection on the night of July 8, in which they would kill their owners' families; they would then march into the backcountry, destroying each White family house by house as they went, and where they would be met by armed representatives of the colonial government, who would help them settle into their own free territory. How much of these accounts were the result of torture inflicted while responding to a set of questions that may or may not have been designed to bring about particular answers is unclear, particularly in regards to any anticipated role played by the Martin administration. It is worth noting that in rounding up captives, many were armed, and the Pitt militia recovered "considerable ammunition." [Quoted from John Simpson to Richard Cogdell, July 15, 1775, William Laurence Saunders, ed. *Colonial Records of North Carolina*, series one (Raleigh, 1886) 10:94–95.]

July 18, 1775

Col. Robert Howe and his militia command marched into Fort Johnston on this night and burned the fort. Gov. Martin witnessed the event from the decks of HMS *Cruizer*, where he had taken refuge.

July 20, 1775

News of Bunker Hill reached Britain, causing conflict between the Whig and Tory political factions regarding the justness of the Patriot cause.

August 14, 1775

The Tryon Resolves were issued. Similar to the Mecklenburg Resolves, which they mimicked in structure, and the Liberty Point Resolves, they were passed by the "Association" of Tryon County (formed of lands west of the Catawba River, with a county seat in what became Lincolnton).

August 20–September 10, 1775

The Third Provincial Congress met in Hillsborough. It decided that North Carolina would supply its proportional number of troops and money to the Continental Army that had been assigned by the Second Continental Congress. On the motion of Richard Caswell, Samuel Johnston was elected president of the Third Provincial Congress. It organized the Committee of Safety, a body that would oversee the formation of civil government throughout the colony, and a Provincial Council to oversee the management of the colony when the Provincial Congress was not in session. The first president of the Provincial Council was Cornelius Harnett.

August 21, 1775

Having arrived in London, Richard Penn Jr. and Arthur Lee presented a copy of the Olive Branch petition to William Legge, 2nd Earl of Dartmouth, Secretary of State to the Colonies and First Lord of Trade.

August 23, 1775

In response to Bunker Hill, George III issued "A Proclamation for Suppressing Rebellion and Sedition," formally declaring the North American colonies to be in a state of rebellion and calling for British forces to put it down.

August 25, 1775–May 6, 1776

Patriot Invasion of Quebec Province, the first offensive action launched by the Patriots in the war. Two columns under the commands of Brig. Gen. Richard Montgomery and Col. Benedict Arnold advanced from Fort Ticonderoga and Massachusetts with the goal of uniting at Quebec City. Both columns encountered delays and lost many of their troops to desertion and enlistment expirations during the difficult marches. The united force launched a night attack on Quebec on December 31 which was repulsed, with Montgomery killed. Arnold's resultant siege of Quebec proved tenuous and was broken by British and Hessian reinforcements on May 6, 1776. The remnants of the Patriot force reached Crown Point on Lake Champlain on July 2. Sir Guy Carleton, governor of Quebec Province, haphazardly pursued the Patriot forces but returned to Quebec to take care of administrative matters and gather enough boats to transfer his army south. The campaign was a disaster for the Patriots and marked their first major defeat in the war. They were unable to mount a campaign against Quebec again.

September 1–2, 1775

In a last effort to avoid a final breach, Penn and Lee presented the original of the Olive Branch Petition to Dartmouth, but upon being informed that the king refused to read it, wrote to Congress on the following day that it had been rejected.

September 1, 1775

Responding to the Second Continental Congress' call for the province to organize two regiments for service in the Continental Army, the Third N.C. Provincial Congress authorized their creation. These would become the 1st and 2nd North Carolina Continental Regiments. There seems to be some confusion as to their original status, as the minutes of the Provincial Congress indicated that the units were regiments and considered part of the Continental force, while the November 28 entry in the journal of the Continental Congress indicated that the units were previously considered to be battalions and provincial forces but were now to be granted Continental status and put on the Continental Army payment system. It would appear that both Congresses used the terms "battalion" and "regiment" interchangeably.

Mid-September 1775

The Admiralty's July order to seize and detain ships reached American waters, and British naval vessels began to put it into effect.

October 1775–March 1776

The first, second, and third formations of the North Carolina Provincial Council oversaw North Carolina's government during this period, dealing with issues concerning Loyalists in the Cape Fear region, the Battle of Moore's Creek Bridge, and sending troops to southeastern Virginia in the Great Bridge campaign.

October 11, 1775

Gen. Thomas Gage set sail for England. He was replaced as commander-in-chief of British forces in North America by Gen. William Howe.

October 27, 1775

George III read a speech to mark the opening of a new Parliament. The King's speech reinforced and amplified upon the points made in his

A Continental soldier from North Carolina, 1775. Illustration by Stephen Marchesi.

August 23 proclamation regarding the colonies being in a state of rebellion and the need to use force to crush it.

November 7, 1775

Governor Dunmore of Virginia signed what became known as Dunmore's Proclamation. It was publicly issued on November 15. It promised freedom for enslaved persons belonging to Patriot enslavers if they ran away and joined the royalist military forces. The proclamation sparked outrage among Patriot slaveholders in Virginia and in neighboring colonies, including North Carolina, where fears of a potential insurrection remained strong following various alarms and rumors throughout the summer.

November 10, 1775

George Germain, 1st Viscount Sackville, became Secretary of State for the Colonies in the administration of Lord North.

November 16–21, 1775

The British sloops *Cruizer* and *Scorpion* were ordered to salvage whatever guns and ammunition remained at Fort Johnston. While the British loaded the guns onto a transport, the *Cruizer* fired at militiamen concealed in the woods surrounding the fort. A party of forty sailors and marines were sent into the fort as a temporary garrison while the operation continued. Armed with swivel guns and muskets, they kept a steady fire into the Patriots and kept them at bay.

November 17, 1775–January 25, 1776

The Knox Expedition (the Noble Train of Artillery); part of the Siege of Boston. Gen. George Washington dispatched Col. Henry Knox to Fort Ticonderoga to bring the cannon captured there to Boston. The Patriot column moved southward in late December, dragging the guns on sledges through often snowy weather, before arriving at Boston in late January.

November 19–21, 1775

The First Siege of Ninety-Six (Savage's Old Fields), South Carolina. A mixed Patriot force from South Carolina, Georgia, and North Carolina, under the command of Maj. Andrew Williamson of the Ninety-Six Regiment of South Carolina militia confronted a force of almost 1,900

Loyalists led by Maj. Joseph Robinson of the Ninety-Six District Loyalist militia.

The size of the Patriot force is unknown; although made up primarily of South Carolinians, it included at least seven companies of the 1st Rowan County Regiment of militia, under the command of Col. Griffith Rutherford. The clash came about when Williamson led his force to recapture ammunition and gunpowder seized by the Loyalists in October. Arriving at Ninety-Six, he established a fortified position which was soon besieged by Robinson. Most of the fighting occurred on November 19, during a sharp skirmish lasting over two hours which was precipitated when two of Williamson's men, seeking water, were captured by the Loyalists during a parley. On November 21, terms were negotiated which allowed Williamson and his men to withdraw safely on the following day. The munitions captured by the Loyalists remained in their hands, but an expedition was soon launched under South Carolina militia Col. Richard Richardson to make another effort.

December 6, 1775

The Second Continental Congress formally responded to the king's August 23 proclamation, reaffirming colonial loyalty to the crown but arguing that Parliament had never had true authority over them because the colonies were not represented in that body, and averring that Congress would continue to resist Parliament while hoping to avoid a full-scale civil war. Nevertheless, the king's proclamation and speech declaring the colonies as being in a state of rebellion had effectively undermined the peace party within Congress.

December 8–30, 1775

The Snow Campaign, S.C. Prior to the First Siege of Ninety-Six, the South Carolina Council of Safety ordered Col. Richard Richardson of the Camden militia to recapture the gunpowder and ammunition taken by the Loyalists in October. While Richardson was gathering a force, Maj. Joseph Robinson decided to recapture the munitions and, as noted above, was stopped at the First Siege of Ninety-Six. By the time of the latter clash, Richardson was on the move into the South Carolina backcountry with about 1,000 men. Halting at the Congaree River on November 27 and on the Enoree River in early December, Richardson gathered more men, his force soon reaching 3,000. This included Col. Griffith Rutherford and his contingent from the 1st Rowan County Regiment of militia,

Members of the North Carolina Militia, such as those who participated in the Snow Campaign in South Carolina in December 1775. Illustration by Stephen Marchesi.

fresh from the Siege of Ninety-Six, as well as other contingents of North Carolina militia, including detachments from the Mecklenburg County militia, the New Berne District militia, and the Tryon County militia. In all, including Rutherford's men, they totaled around 900 North Carolina militiamen along with some 200 men from the 1st and 2nd North Carolina Continental Regiments. By December 8, Richardson was on the march again, capturing Loyalists as he went. Word came of a Loyalist camp on the Reedy River, inside Cherokee country. The Loyalists were commanded by Patrick Cunningham, who led the raid which captured the munitions in October. The Patriot leaders were greatly concerned that a possible alliance between the British and the Loyalists would develop with the Cherokee; indeed, the arms and ammunition captured in October had originally been intended as a gift to the Cherokee as a pacifying gesture. On December 21, Richardson sent 1,300 men under the command of Col. William Thomson, including a contingent from the 2nd North Carolina Continental Regiment under future governor Lt. Col. Alexander Martin, to strike Cunningham. The Patriots surprised the Loyalists in camp at the Battle of Great Cane Brake the following day. The Loyalists were routed and the munitions recaptured, although Cunningham escaped. Casualties were light on both sides, with many of the Loyalists taken prisoner. On December 23, a heavy snowstorm struck and hit the Patriots, who lacked winter clothing and tents. The weather continued bad as the reunited Patriot force marched to the coast, arriving on December 30. Richardson declared his campaign successful and felt that the chance of the Cherokee going to war on the Loyalist side was ended. The following year proved him wrong.

December 9, 1775

The Battle of Great Bridge, Virginia. Lord Dunmore ordered a fortification built at the bridge over the Elizabeth River, in the midst of the Great Dismal Swamp, to block access to Norfolk from North Carolina. The fort was occupied by elements of the British 14th Regiment of Foot and two Virginia Loyalist regiments, the Ethiopian Regiment, made up of African Americans who had enlisted as a result of Dunmore's November proclamation, and the Queen's Own Loyal Virginia Regiment. Col. William Woodford of the 2nd Virginia Regiment of the Virginia provisional forces was sent to oppose the Royalist advance. He established a camp on the opposite side of the bridge on December 2. Over the next few days, he was joined by men from Virginia and North Carolina. The latter included 150 members of the Halifax District Minutemen Battalion led by Col. Nicholas Long.

Dunmore ordered an attack on the Patriot position on December 9, due to rumors that they had brought up artillery (guns had arrived, but they were dismounted and therefore inoperable). One company each of British grenadiers and naval gunners advanced across the bridge and stormed the Patriot earthworks, but while the contingents of the Queen's Own supported them with fire from the opposite bank, the contingents of the Ethiopian Regiment had been sent on another mission and were not present. The attacking column was driven back with heavy casualties in a fight that lasted about a half hour. The 2nd North Carolina Continental Regiment under Col. Robert Howe, minus a detachment dispatched to South Carolina, arrived to reinforce Woodford on the following day. Howe, as a Continental Army officer, outranked Woodford and assumed command of the Patriot force. The Patriot victory at Great Bridge made the British abandon Norfolk. Dunmore and his men took refuge on British ships anchored in the port's harbor, accompanied by the Tory residents of the town. The British defeat dampened immediate prospects of a slave insurrection in southeastern Virginia and northeastern North Carolina. Howe and his command are sometimes represented in secondary sources as having participated in the fighting at Great Bridge, with Howe sometimes even depicted as the Patriot commander in the action, but these claims are inaccurate.

December 22, 1775

Parliament passed the Prohibitory Act, which forbade all commerce between Britain and the thirteen colonies and established a formal blockade. Since blockades were considered to be formal acts of war, the law tacitly acknowledged the true state of affairs between Britain and the colonies. The law went into effect the following March.

January 1, 1776

The burning of Norfolk, Virginia. Having occupied Norfolk on December 14, Robert Howe and William Woodford concluded that retaining control of the port was untenable, as the mobility provided by the British warships risked their being cut off and captured. They thus recommended to the Virginia House of Burgesses that they abandon Norfolk and evacuate its remaining inhabitants after it was rendered unfit for British use. While waiting for a response, Howe refused to allow the British to purchase provisions in the town, even after four warships lined up facing the docks. Adding insult to injury, Howe ordered the Patriot force to parade daily along the Norfolk waterfront, including a changing of the guard ceremony. Despite a warning from Capt. Henry Bellew of the HMS *Liverpool* regarding both the provisions and the daily military ceremony, Howe refused to yield on either point. Late on the afternoon of January 1, the four British warships opened fire on Norfolk, commencing a bombardment that lasted until after dark. Small parties of British troops and sailors went ashore to capture provisions and set fire to buildings which the Patriots had been using to snipe at the British squadron. Soon much of the waterfront was on fire. The Patriots drove off the landing parties but did little to stop the fires, and even added to them, as they targeted properties known to belong to Loyalists. Soon discipline broke down into general chaos as the Patriot militia began to generally loot and burn the town, carrying on for the next three days until Howe regained control. In his subsequent report to the Burgesses, Howe omitted the role played by the Patriot forces in the destruction of much of Norfolk and publicly assigned blame to the British, although rumors about the truth of the matter soon circulated. Meanwhile, Howe's plan for the reduction of Norfolk was approved by the Burgesses, and by early February the rest of Norfolk had been destroyed by the Patriots.

January 8, 1776

In anticipation that New York City would be Sir William Howe's target in 1776, Washington ordered Maj. Gen. Charles Lee to the city to survey its defenses and strengthen them. Working through March, Lee constructed a defensive network designed to make any British attack so costly that it would force the King, Cabinet, and Parliament to come to terms with the colonists, leading to reconciliation on the Patriots' terms.

January 16, 1776

The Continental Congress authorized the raising of a third "battalion" in North Carolina that became the 3rd North Carolina Continental Regiment.

February 27, 1776

The Continental Congress established what would later be officially titled the Southern Department of the Continental Army, which oversaw all Continental forces operating in the provinces (and later, states) of Virginia, North Carolina, South Carolina, and Georgia, and the lands of their western frontiers.

February 27, 1776

The Battle of Moores Creek Bridge, the first major battle of the war fought in North Carolina. As part of the effort to reestablish royal authority in North Carolina, Gov. Josiah Martin proposed to rouse a large Loyalist force if it could be armed and supported by a force of British regulars. Gen. Sir William Howe and his brother, Adm. Richard Lord Howe, approved an expedition of British troops that would unite with the Loyalists at Brunswick in mid-February. The plan began to unravel, however, as the Loyalists decided to muster and march before they were fully gathered. Unfortunately for the Loyalists, bad weather scattered the British ships transporting the troops and their escorting warships, and they did not arrive until May. Many of the Loyalists were Scottish emigrants or their descendants who had come to North Carolina in the years following the suppression of the 1745 Jacobite Rebellion. It is thus somewhat ironic that they fought for the British Crown, as was the fact that they were accompanied for part of their march by ardent Jacobite nationalist Flora MacDonald. On February 27, the rival forces confronted each other at the Widow Moores' Bridge crossing of Moores Creek, a Cape Fear tributary, on the road leading north from Wilmington eighteen miles to the south. The Patriots initially occupied trenches on either side of the creek, but prior to the Loyalist attempt on the bridge, those on the west bank withdrew to reinforce their comrades on the east bank. The Loyalists attempted to force a crossing with an attack by Scotsmen armed only with broadswords, but they found the bridge planking removed. As they struggled to get across, they were hit by musket and artillery fire from the Patriots and quickly routed. The Patriots replaced the planking and crossed the bridge, charging the Loyalists, who fled the field. The whole fight lasted perhaps as much as three minutes. Out of some 1,100 Patriots engaged, only one was killed and one wounded, while out of some 1,800 Loyalists there were thirty killed, twenty wounded, and 850 captured. Although hardly a battle in the sense of the amount of time elapsed, Moores Creek Bridge still proved important because it ended direct British/Loyalist threats to North Carolina for several years.

A Loyalist Highlander. Many Scottish Highland immigrants to North Carolina supported the British government during the Revolution, 1776. Illustration by Stephen Marchesi.

March 1, 1776

The Prohibitory Act went into effect, marking the beginning of a full blockade of the thirteen colonies by the Royal Navy.

March 1, 1776

The Continental Congress elected Col. James Moore of the 1st North Carolina Continental Regiment and Col. Robert Howe of the 2nd North Carolina Continental Regiment as brigadier generals in the Continental Line. The Congress also appointed Maj. Gen. Charles Lee as the first commander of the Southern Department of the Continental Army.

March 3–4, 1776

The Patriots raided Nassau in the Bahamas to capture gunpowder and other military supplies originally housed at Williamsburg, Virginia, but moved to the island in 1775 by order of Lord Dunmore to prevent their possible seizure by the Patriots. When the Patriot forces landed, the British evacuated most of the gunpowder by ship. The Patriots gathered up the remaining gunpowder and whatever other military supplies that they could take before departing. The expedition marked the first landing of what would become the United States Marine Corps and foreshadowed the later importance of the Caribbean following France's entry into the war in 1778.

March 4, 1776

The Continental Army occupied Dorchester Heights, overlooking Boston and its harbor, and fortified it with the artillery brought by Knox from Fort Ticonderoga. British plans to dislodge the Patriots failed due to the weather, and as the guns on the heights could hit supply ships entering the port, Sir William Howe was forced to make the decision to evacuate Boston.

March 4, 1776

During a meeting of the North Carolina Provincial Council (February 28–March 5, 1776), an important step was taken in the direction of imposing loyalty oaths on citizens. The council approved a resolution in which those disarmed on the orders of the local Committee of Safety were required to "swear on the holy Evangelists of Almighty God" that during the current crisis they were not to oppose, either peacefully or militarily, the measures

A citizen swearing an oath. Loyalty oaths were eventually imposed on North Carolina citizens by the Patriot government as part of the effort to stamp out Loyalist support in the state. Illustration by Stephen Marchesi.

of the Continental Congress or the Provincial Congress, or any troops raised by them, nor were they to offer support to any officers of the Crown. Likewise, they were not to try to persuade their fellow citizens to support the positions of Parliament over those of the congresses.

March 12, 1776

The portion of the British expedition to the South carrying troops from Boston arrived in the Cape Fear River. It was commanded by Maj. Gen. Sir Henry Clinton. While anchored in the river, seventy-one enslaved freedom seekers reached the British fleet. Clinton organized them into a company called the Black Pioneers, commanded by White commissioned officers but with Black noncommissioned officers. The company performed physical labor for the British soldiers, including clearing roads and spaces for campsites.

March 17, 1776

The British forces in Boston evacuated by sea, along with many Loyalists who fled to the port. The fleet carrying the troops sailed to Nova Scotia, where the British regrouped and planned their next move. The end of the siege marked a major victory for the Patriot side, although the success soon proved brief.

March 22, 1776

In retaliation for the Prohibitory Act, the Second Continental Congress authorized privateering. Privateering was an old naval practice that lay somewhere in between the realm of regular naval operations and criminal piracy. Private individuals were granted commissions called letters of marque from their government which gave them the authority to use a private vessel to capture enemy ships. As privateers were usually granted a share of the profits from the sale of captured cargos, their targets would usually be enemy merchant vessels, rather than naval ships of war, although the latter could also be taken. North Carolina contributed its own share of privateers to the Revolution, with wealthy merchantmen such as John Wright Stanley outfitting several vessels. In addition, Loyalist privateers attacked Patriot vessels off the Carolina coast.

Freedom seekers searching for safety. There were many different quests for freedom during the Revolutionary era, and enslaved persons owned by Patriot supporters often sought their own freedom by fleeing to the British, who frequently offered freedom in exchange for their support in the war effort. Some enlisted to fight on the British side. Illustration by Stephen Marchesi.

March 26, 1776

The Continental Congress resolved that if North Carolina's "convention or committee of safety" believed it was "necessary for the common safety to raise one or two more batallions [sic]," then they would be put into Continental service once they were mustered and equipped.

April 4–May 14, 1776

The Fourth North Carolina Provincial Congress met in Halifax. Samuel Johnston was elected its president. On April 8, Thomas Burke, Cornelius Harnett, Allen Jones, Thomas Jones, John Kinchen, Abner Nash, and Thomas Person were appointed to a committee to draft a resolution concerning the idea of independence in the face of what they perceived as the wrong actions of the King.

April 4, 1776

Washington began shifting his army from Boston to New York in anticipation of an attack by Sir William Howe's British army.

April 6–27, 1776

At Brunswick Town, there was frequent skirmishing between British landing parties from Clinton's expedition and a mixed command of North Carolina Continental soldiers and militia under the command of Brig. Gen. James Moore. The British picked up refugees from the Moores Creek defeat, as well as enslaved freedom seekers belonging to Patriot owners, while foraging off the locals.

April 9, 1776

The North Carolina Provincial Congress used the authorizations of the Continental Congress in January to raise a new "battalion" (regiment) and "one or two more" in March to order the raising of four regiments: the 3rd, 4th, 5th, and 6th North Carolina Continental Regiments. Regimental officers were appointed by the Provincial Congress on April 15.

April 12, 1776

The committee from the Fourth North Carolina Provincial Congress issued what became known as the Halifax Resolves. The Resolves called upon the colony's representatives at the Second Continental Congress to vote for independence in conjunction with their colleagues from other colonies, and to form foreign alliances, while reserving for North Carolina

Members of the Fourth North Provincial Congress discuss the Halifax Resolves, which authorized North Carolina's representatives at the Second Continental Congress to vote for independence alongside their colleagues from other colonies. It was the first time that the government of a British colony formally advocated for independence. Illustration by Stephen Marchesi.

the exclusive right to make its own laws and create its own constitution. This marked the first instance of a British colony formally advocating for independence, albeit within the context of a hypothetical joint action taken with delegates from other colonies.

April 12, 1776

The first ships from the fleet from England, earlier scattered in stormy weather, began to arrive in the Cape Fear River and united with Clinton. The naval contingent was commanded by Adm. Sir Peter Parker.

April 29–May 13, 1776

The Fourth North Carolina Provincial Congress issued resolutions involving Loyalists captured during the Moores Creek campaign. On April 29 the Congress approved a declaration concerning Loyalists prisoners considered enough of a threat to the general peace that they were exiled from their areas of residence. The declaration averred that the Patriot government would not persecute the families of the Loyalists left behind, and held out the hope that the prisoners would eventually realize that they were wrong, seek reconciliation and embrace the Patriot cause. On May 1, the Congress passed a resolution appointing commissioners for Guilford, Cumberland, Anson, Orange, Bladen and Chatham Counties to inventory the estates of the Loyalist prisoners from these counties, to prevent the estates from mismanagement and waste, to look after the interests of the women and children of the households, and to prevent the seizure of any property except for arms and ammunition. On the same day, the Congress passed a resolution authorizing Cumberland County to dispose of the estate of a deceased Loyalist. On May 13, the Congress passed a resolution that anyone in the future who took up arms against America within North Carolina or offered aid to the British would, upon conviction by the Congress or the judiciary, forfeit all of their property to the people of North Carolina. These measures laid the foundations for a loyalty oath to the colony and culminated in the establishment of a confiscation law for the property of North Carolina Loyalists.

May 1776

In the spring of 1775, French playwright Pierre-Augustin Caron de Beaumarchais ("The Barber of Seville"and "The Marriage of Figaro") was sent to London to recover private royal correspondence from an alienated former French diplomat who threatened to publish them. While in

Britain, Beaumarchais became friends with John Wilkes and other Britons sympathetic to the American cause and soon began to lobby his nation's government to help the colonists on the argument that the discomfit of British interests would accrue to French advantage. By the spring of 1776, the French government had been swayed by Beaumarchais' arguments and began to work secretly with its close ally, Spain (both countries were ruled by different branches of the French Bourbon dynasty), to bring aid to the revolutionaries. In May 1776, these efforts bore fruit with the organization of a corporation called Roderigue Hortalez and Company, which was designed to secretly funnel arms and munitions to the rebellious Americans while operating as a legitimate business. Beaumarchais was the company's director under the guise of the fictitious Hortalez. Over the next few years, Hortalez and Company supplied weapons, gunpowder, uniforms, and other military necessities to the Patriot government through multiple clandestine methods.

May 1–3, 1776

Elements of the British fleet continued to arrive in the Cape Fear River. Maj. Gen. Sir Henry Clinton ordered the destruction of Fort Johnston, due to it being a haven for Patriot snipers. On May 3, reinforcements from Ireland, under the command of Maj. Gen. Charles Cornwallis, 1st Marquess Cornwallis, reached the Cape Fear, at last completing the forces intended for the Southern expedition.

May 1, 1776

The Fourth North Carolina Provincial Congress appointed William Hooper, Joseph Hewes, and John Penn to represent North Carolina in the Second Continental Congress. These three would be the North Carolina signers of the Declaration of Independence.

May 5, 1776

From aboard the transport ship HMS *Palliser* anchored in the Cape Fear River, Sir Henry Clinton issued a proclamation offering a pardon to all rebellious North Carolinians who would lay down their weapons and reaffirm their allegiance to the crown. Exempted from the pardon were Cornelius Harnett and Robert Howe. The proclamation also called for the dissolution of the Provincial Congress, all Committees of Safety and similar extralegal bodies, and for judges to be allowed to resume holding court.

May 11, 1776

Skirmish at Orton Mill and Kendall Plantation, near the Cape Fear River in Brunswick County. Clinton personally led a raid in the direction of the bridge at Orton Mill. Moving by boat, the British first stopped at Kendall Plantation, home of Patriot Gen. Robert Howe. Militia sentries fired on the British and departed. At the plantation, the British reached the main house and found only women of the Howe family in residence—one was shot in the hip, another bayonetted, and a third butted with a musket. They later received financial compensation from Clinton and Cornwallis for their mistreatment. Suffering casualties from militiamen firing from concealment, the British pushed on to the mill, burned it, and retreated to their boats, ransacking houses along the way.

May 17, 1776

Cornwallis led 900 British regulars on a night raid to Brunswick Town, hoping to catch the Patriot forces reputedly based there. They skirmished with guards and quickly occupied the town, finding it had been abandoned by both soldiers and inhabitants.

June 5, 1776

Another step toward a loyalty oath for North Carolina citizens was made on this day, during the session of the North Carolina Council of Safety (June 5–July 16, 1776). Brig. Gen. John Ashe of the North Carolina militia reported to the council concerning "a number of outlying malcontents" in Bladen County who wished to return home and were willing to submit to the judgement of the Council of Safety. The Council imposed an oath on the individuals in question, involved in "the late insurrection" (probably the Moores Creek Bridge campaign), which would be given before the chairman of the Council, requiring them to obey the regulations of the Patriot government of the colony, and to serve in the defense of the colony when required. In exchange, they would be allowed to go home.

June 9, 1776

Having regrouped and been reinforced in Nova Scotia following the withdrawal from Boston, British Maj. Gen. Sir William Howe planned a new offensive, this time against the port of New York, as Washington had anticipated. The expedition was jointly commanded by Howe and his brother, Rear Adm. Richard Howe, 1st Earl Howe and

Commander-in-Chief of the Royal Navy's North American Station. The first contingent of the expedition departed Halifax under General Howe on this date.

Summer 1776

Maj. Gen. Charles Lee, commander of the Southern Department of the Continental Army, dispatched two officers to New Orleans to ask for aid from the governor of Spanish Louisiana, Luis de Unzaga y Amézaga. Unzaga agreed to secretly supply five tons of gunpowder to the Patriots. This marked the beginning of a clandestine supply network from New Orleans which provided much needed assistance to the struggling Patriots. Unzaga was related to the House of Gardoqui, and New Orleans soon became a focal point of Díego de Gardiqui's supply operations, as well as those of the French-run Hortalez and Company.

June 28, 1776

Having decided that North Carolina was not ripe territory for British operations in the wake of Moores Creek Bridge, Clinton, Parker, and Cornwallis selected Charleston, South Carolina as a target. On June 28, the British attacked Sullivan's Island, in Charleston Harbor.

The subsequent attempt to reduce Fort Sullivan, the primary fortification guarding the island, by naval bombardment failed, and the British fleet was badly shot up. A contingent of 750 men from the 1st North Carolina Continental Regiment under Lt. Col. Thomas Clark was part of the force manning the various Charleston defenses, but they were stationed near Haddrell's Point on the mainland north of Sullivan's Island and did not participate in the battle.

July 2, 1776–January 6, 1777

The New York and New Jersey Campaign was the major military campaign of 1776. The British under Sir William Howe captured New York City, defeated Washington's army in a series of battles, and drove it into Pennsylvania. Washington, however, launched two raids across the Delaware River into New Jersey in the winter of 1776–1777 that resulted in two Patriot victories at a time when support for the war effort was fading among many.

July 2, 1776

British forces began landing unopposed on Staten Island. Sir William Howe's command included the British troops from the siege of Boston and fresh arrivals from Britain, as well as Hessian mercenaries recruited from various German provinces.

July 4, 1776

The Declaration of Independence was ratified by the Second Continental Congress.

North Carolina's signers of the Declaration of Independence:
Joseph Hewes (*left*), William Hooper (*right*), and John Penn Penn (*bottom*). Joseph Hewes, unknown artist, date of painting unknown, Guilford Courthouse National Military Park, accessed March 26, 2026; https://commons.wikimedia.org/wiki/File:Joseph_Hewes.png ; William Hooper, unknown artist, date of painting unknown, Guilford Courthouse National Military Park, accessed March 26, 2026; https://commons.wikimedia.org/wiki/File:William_Hooper.png; John Penn, unkwown artist, date of painting unknown, Guilford Courthouse National Military Park, accessed March 26, 2026; https://commons.wikimedia.org/wiki/File:John_Penn_Guilford_Courthouse.png .

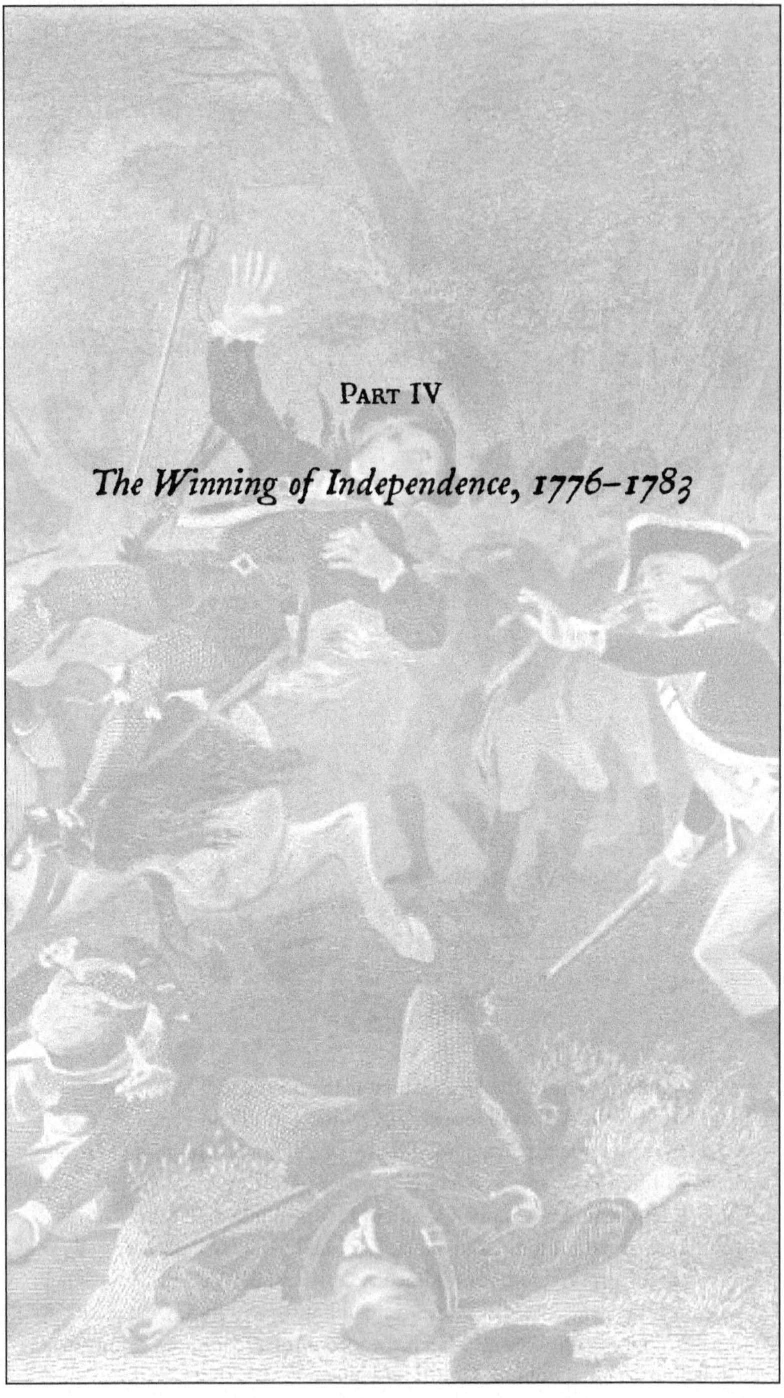

Part IV

The Winning of Independence, 1776–1783

The American Revolutionary War, like any major conflict lasting several years, underwent several phases, but to simplify matters will be divided here into two major periods. The first phase, beginning over a year before the Declaration of Independence and ending in early 1778, involved British efforts to subdue the Northern and Mid-Atlantic colonies (later states), starting with the initial fighting in Massachusetts and ending with the great Patriot victory at Saratoga, in New York in 1777. This was followed by the diplomatic maneuvers that led to France making a military alliance with the new republic. Part of this phase has already been covered in Part III. Initially, the Patriots responded aggressively to Lexington and Concord. They acted energetically to besiege Boston and conquer Canada. This brought mixed results, as the British were forced to evacuate Boston, while the Patriot invasion of Canada failed miserably. Soon, however, the British were reinforced and they went on the offensive, mounting campaigns that resulted in the capture of New York City and the Patriot capital of Philadelphia. The British were unable to destroy Washington's army, however. In the period between the New York and Philadelphia operations, Washington was able to mount a short winter campaign in New Jersey which netted small victories and kept Patriot morale going. The Patriot battle of Saratoga, when a Patriot army defeated a British drive south from Canada, occurred simultaneously with the campaigning in Pennsylvania and proved a major setback for the British. It not only demonstrated that the British could be beaten, but exposed the weaknesses in British strategy and leadership, as the lack of coordination between the Philadelphia and Saratoga campaigns contributed directly to the failure of the latter operation. It also had major repercussions diplomatically, as the United States forged a military alliance with France that brought Britain's oldest and most formidable foe into the war.

The widening of the war into a major international conflict opened the final phase of the conflict. In North America, the British were forced to retrench, as they were no longer able to send major reinforcements to the main army. They abandoned Philadelphia and withdrew to New York. This occurred at a time when Washington's army, having received training in European tactics, was able to operate as a more professional force and challenged the British on the field of battle more successfully. But although the British still sought victory in North America, they needed a new approach to achieve that goal. The entrance of France into the war in 1778 on the side of the United States, followed by the 1779 entrance of Spain on the side of France, and Britain's decision to declare war upon the Dutch in 1780, meant the Britain had to defend the rest of its empire from attack. The British also saw an opportunity to grab territory at the expense of its foes. Thus, fighting raged around the globe, particularly in the West Indies, the seat of major colonies of all four powers, as well as in Gibraltar and the Mediterranean, India, the coast of Africa, the Pacific, and the Gulf of Mexico. It is beyond the scope of this chronology to cover all of the campaigns and battles around the world between 1778 and 1783 between Britain and its European rivals, but it has included several of the more important ones in order to illustrate the immensity of the conflict and the strain that it imposed on British military resources, a strain that played a major role in Britain's ultimate defeat. It is also a side of the American Revolutionary War that is little known to most Americans today, but a knowledge of which is important to fully understand the story of the winning of American independence.

With the widening of the international side of the war, the British forces in North America sought a path to victory that involved doing more with less resources. In London, the British government believed that the road to retake the rebellious colonies was through the implementation of what has become known as the "Southern strategy." The plan was based heavily around the belief that the majority of the White inhabitants in the South remained loyal to the Crown and only needed a strong showing by British military forces in order to rise up, organize, and assist the British in reclaiming control of the region. The idea was for the British to establish a strong base within a particular Southern colony (state) and organize the Loyalists into militia. The Loyalists would then assume control of the colony, while the British marched north into the next colony to repeat the process. The British hoped they could gain control of at least the Carolinas through this method, and possibly Virginia as well. If successful, they would force the rebel government to come to terms; or, if that failed, they would at least have regained the agriculturally rich South, with its close economic ties to Britain's Caribbean colonies, and left a weakened United States that could be easily dominated by a victorious Britain.

The belief that the South was dominated by Loyalists, which underlay the Southern strategy, was based on a mixture of fact and fiction, and unfortunately for the British it was mostly fiction. It was true that there were more Loyalists in the South than in the North, but they did not constitute a majority of the White population. Furthermore, by the time the British got around to forming the Southern strategy, the Loyalist population was largely cowed due to years of repression by Patriot militia forces. British officers found that the Loyalists might come out if they were in the area, but they would not organize unless the British troops stayed permanently

A Cherokee Middletown village. The Middle Cherokee villages lay east of the Appalachians. Illustration by Stephen Marchesi.

with them, undermining the plan for the Loyalists to assume control while the British moved on. The Southern strategy was thus based on false premises caused by the gap between official belief and reality and thus faced major problems for achieving success from the start.

Nevertheless, the British established bases in Georgia and South Carolina and used the latter as their springboard for subduing the rest of the region. Unfortunately for the British, their commander in South Carolina, Lord Cornwallis, largely ignored his instructions to secure South Carolina before moving into North Carolina. He launched two invasions into North Carolina while the situation was still unsettled in South Carolina. Both of these invasions ended in failure: the first, when a force screening his flank was destroyed at Kings Mountain; and the second, due to a debilitating campaign that took the British far from their supply base. They were unable to achieve a decisive victory over their Patriot foes. Instead, their major engagement with the Patriots at Guilford Courthouse in North Carolina was a pyrrhic victory, with the Patriot force withdrawing intact while leaving a quarter of Cornwallis's army killed and wounded. Cornwallis, floundering around for some solution, decided to march to Virginia where he was forced to surrender at Yorktown, leading to the end of the war. His opponent, Nathanael Greene, marched into South Carolina and began the slow process of driving the British from the various posts that they held in that state. Thus, the Southern strategy proved to be the ruin of Britain's hopes for regaining at least part of their rebellious colonies.

July 21, 1776

The British expedition to the South departed the Carolinas to participate in the New York campaign.

August–November, 1776

A series of expeditions by Patriot forces was waged against the Cherokee Indians. The background of the conflict was the continuing White expansion into the area, as settlers encroached more and more on traditional Cherokee grounds. This led to raids on settlements by the Cherokee, which sparked the expeditions as retaliation. In addition, the British openly courted the Cherokee as allies against the Patriots, and some Loyalist Whites accompanied the Cherokee on their raids. On August 1, a force from South Carolina and Georgia under Col. Andrew Williamson began to attack Cherokee villages in South Carolina before pushing northward into North Carolina in mid-September. There, they were to rendezvous with North Carolina forces under the command of Gen. Griffith Rutherford. Although Rutherford did not fully muster until mid-October, he and the men he had available united with Williamson in late September. Williamson soon returned to South Carolina after destroying several Cherokee villages. Between mid-October and mid-November, Rutherford's column was on the move, destroying more villages. Another force, from Virginia, and under the command of Col. William Christian, also crossed into North Carolina and destroyed more villages in western North Carolina and what is now eastern Tennessee. In May and July 1777, the devastated Cherokee signed treaties with the colonists, ending the fighting for the present (see below).

August 9, 1776

The Fourth North Carolina Provincial Council met and appointed first Samuel Ashe and then, after Ashe's resignation, Willie Jones as head of the newly named Council of Safety. Jones was therefore executive of the state until Richard Caswell became governor.

August 22, 1776

Clinton and Cornwallis, recently arrived from South Carolina, landed troops on Long Island (New York and New Jersey Campaign).

August 27, 1776

The British defeated the Patriots at the Battle of Long Island. Washington's men withdrew to fortifications on Brooklyn Heights (New York and New Jersey Campaign).

August 29–30, 1776

As the British constructed entrenchments which gradually brought them closer to the Patriot fortifications on Brooklyn Heights, the Continental Army was in an untenable position with its back against the East River. Washington ordered a withdrawal to Manhattan Island on this night (New York and New Jersey Campaign).

September 9, 1776

Brig. Gen. James Moore of North Carolina was appointed commander of the Southern Department of the Continental Army, replacing Maj. Gen. Charles Lee, who was recalled to Washington's army in the midst of the New York campaign.

September 11, 1776

In the wake of the British victory on Long Island, Admiral Howe proposed a peace meeting with Patriot representatives, which took place on Staten Island on this date. Howe met with three members of the Continental Congress: John Adams, Benjamin Franklin, and Edward Rutledge. Although Howe hoped to arrange a peace settlement, the meeting was doomed from the start, as the Congressmen were given no authority except to ask certain questions and would not allow the consideration of broader issues without British recognition of American independence, which Howe could not grant. On his part, Howe was not authorized to repeal any policies that were onerous to the Patriots. After about three hours, the conference ended inconclusively.

September 15, 1776

After weeks of inactivity, the British landed on Manhattan Island and occupied New York City (New York and New Jersey Campaign).

September 16, 1776

The Patriots defeated the British at the Battle of Harlem Heights (New York and New Jersey Campaign).

September 19, 1776

Skirmish at Black Hole (Coweecho River) between Williamson's expedition that included a contingent of Catawba Indians, and a mixed force of Cherokee and Loyalists.

October 7–November 2, 1776

British counteroffensive from Quebec into New York state. Following his return to Quebec after his pursuit of the defeated Patriot forces, Sir Guy Carleton began the difficult task of transporting ships to the Richelieu River and constructing new ones. He planned to sail his forces to Lake Champlain, which would give him access to the Hudson River and the chance to link up with Sir William Howe's forces in and around New York City, thus isolating the New England states. Benedict Arnold, meanwhile, constructed a flotilla to defend the lake. On October 11, 1776, Carleton and Arnold clashed at the Battle of Valcour Island. Arnold lost most of his ships but escaped with the remainder to Crown Point, which was soon occupied by the British. Carleton failed to take Ticonderoga, however, and after exchanging prisoners, returned to Quebec for the winter. The outcome of Carleton's offensive caused problems for the British in the following year, as Gen. John Burgoyne's 1777 campaign south toward Albany had to start from Canada rather than the advanced post of Ticonderoga.

October 12–21, 1776

On October 12, the British landed forces at Throgs Neck in the Patriot rear in an attempt to trap them on Manhattan. A delaying action by Patriot troops at Pell's Point on October 18 held the British up long enough for Washington to organize an evacuation. Leaving a garrison behind to hold Fort Washington on northern Manhattan Island and Fort Lee across the Hudson River in New Jersey, Washington and his army withdrew to White Plains, north of New York City, on October 21 (New York and New Jersey Campaign).

October 28, 1776

Howe's army defeated Washington's men at White Plains, New York (New York and New Jersey Campaign).

November 12–December 23, 1776

The Fifth North Carolina Provincial Congress met in Halifax. It developed a new state bill of rights and a state constitution, declaring it the law of the land on December 18, 1776, and ordered the formation of a Council of State and a new General Assembly. Richard Caswell was chosen as the new governor of North Carolina. The constitution provided for three separate branches of government and for free elections to both houses of the general assembly. The powers of the governor were limited. Many of the issues that had aroused the ire of colonists, such as the issuance of general warrants, were addressed.

November 16, 1776

Sir William Howe captured Fort Washington on Manhattan Island on this date, forcing the abandonment of Fort Lee, New Jersey, on November 19. Washington afterwards withdrew through New Jersey and across the Delaware River into Pennsylvania, pursued by Cornwallis (New York and New Jersey Campaign).

Richard Caswell, North Carolina's first state governor, chosen by the Fifth Provincial Congress in November 1776. State Archives of North Carolina.

November 26, 1776

The Fifth North Carolina Provincial Congress resolved to raise three more Continental regiments (referred to in the Congressional minutes as "battalions"): the 7th, 8th, and 9th North Carolina Continental Regiments.

December 8, 1776

British forces from New York City under Sir Henry Clinton landed in Rhode Island and seized Newport.

December 25–26, 1776

Battle of Trenton, New Jersey. Near the end of 1776, Washington elected to take the initiative and revive Patriot morale by striking at isolated British and Hessian garrisons across the Delaware River in New Jersey. His army crossed the river on this night and defeated the Hessian garrison at Trenton, which surrendered. The Continental Army then withdrew back into Pennsylvania (New York and New Jersey Campaign).

January 1, 1777

Bernardo de Gálvez became governor of Spanish Louisiana. He continued his predecessor's policy of supplying covert military aid to the United States.

January 3, 1777

Battle of Princeton, New Jersey. Washington recrossed the Delaware River on December 29 and returned to Trenton, where he was attacked by Cornwallis's larger force at Assunpink Creek (or Second Trenton) on January 2. The British were unsuccessful in their efforts to storm the American earthworks, but Cornwallis felt confident that he could entrap Washington's army on the following day. Washington evaded the trap by a night march around Cornwallis's flank with the goal of striking the British garrison at Princeton. The Patriots defeated the British at Princeton on January 3. Washington was forced to withdraw that evening as Cornwallis moved to Princeton with reinforcements. The Continental Army reached Morristown on January 6 and went into winter quarters, while Cornwallis pulled back to New Brunswick, New Jersey. The Battles of Trenton and Princeton resulted in a major boost in morale among the Patriots, whose support for the conflict had been waning steadily as a result of the military setbacks of the summer and fall (New York and New Jersey Campaign).

January 6, 1777

George Washington ordered smallpox inoculation for the soldiers of the Continental Army.

January 16, 1777

Richard Caswell became the first state governor of North Carolina. Tryon Palace, in New Bern, was the temporary state capitol.

March–July 1777

The "Gourd Patch Conspiracy," a plot against the North Carolina state government by a secret society of farmers from Martin, Tyrell, Pitt, and Bertie Counties. Founded by farmer John Lewelling, the society was organized as a result of the state's disestablishment of the Church of England as North Carolina's official religion and was fueled by long-standing animosity toward Catholicism and France that had been common throughout Britain's North American colonies. As rumors spread that the new republic might form an alliance with France in the struggle against Britain, alarmed and devout Anglicans such as Lewelling felt the need to organize to defend Anglicanism from what they believed was a conspiracy of Catholics and atheists dominating the state government. Originally a non-violent organization, the society became increasingly militant under Lewelling's leadership as its members opposed the state

Members of the "Gourd Patch Conspiracy" against the state government meet. Members of the conspiracy were fervent Anglicans who believed that a Catholic and atheist conspiracy dominated North Carolina's government. The group gradually became militant and plotted to overthrow the government, but the conspiracy fell apart as rumors of its existence and plans reached state authorities. Illustration by Stephen Marchesi.

military draft and as the state government required oaths of loyalty from citizens. Lewelling plotted to raid Halifax, where a powder magazine was located, to gain arms and ammunition for his followers. The attack was timed to coincide with the visit of Gov. Richard Caswell to Halifax, who would be either kidnapped or murdered by the plotters. The conspiracy began to unravel when a Chowan County slave patroller, whom Lewelling asked to spread rumors of an imminent slave rebellion to serve as a distraction from the main plot (and perhaps in fact to spark a genuine rebellion; the actual plan remains murky), revealed the existence of an anti-popery scheme to the authorities in June. Two other members of the conspiracy were arrested and more details of the plot revealed. Alarmed, Lewelling held a meeting with other members in a gourd patch (from which the conspiracy later took its name). In this and subsequent meetings, the potential targets of the conspirators expanded, and the group began to shift to a Loyalist conspiracy, as Lewelling decided in early July to contact British army commander Sir William Howe for help. The members assigned to go to Howe turned back due to a lack of funding for their journey, and the authorities by now were fully aware of a plan to seize the powder mill at Halifax. A small band, led by Lewelling, was captured near Tarboro in mid-July, while other members fled. Lewelling was tried and convicted for treason but pardoned by Caswell, the first legal case of clemency in state history. Several other conspirators were granted clemency as well. The story of the conspiracy illustrates the complexities of the Revolution, and the fact that dissent and loyalties did not always fit neatly along a straight Patriot vs. Loyalist spectrum.

April 7, 1777

The first North Carolina state legislature met in New Bern. The General Assembly met twice through the remainder of 1777, from April 7 to May 9, and from November 15 to December 24. It established six new counties: Burke, Camden, Caswell, Nash, Washington (now in Tennessee), and Wilkes. One of the laws passed in the April 7–May 9 session was "An Act to Prevent Domestic Insurrections, and For Other Purposes." The law was prompted largely by the emancipation practices of the Quakers in the backcountry, described in the law as "an evil and pernicious Practice." It put an end to emancipation "except for meritorious Services" as determined by the county courts. Otherwise, enslaved persons who had been emancipated were to be hunted down and arrested by the sheriffs, who would hold them in jail until the next court session, at which point they would be auctioned to the highest bidder. If enslaved persons were allowed to hire themselves out to others by their masters, then they were liable to be arrested and put to hard labor in service of the poor of the county for twenty days. Another important law passed by the legislature during the spring session was "An Act declaring what Crimes and Practices against the State shall be Treason, and providing Punishments adequate to Crimes of both Classes, and for preventing the Dangers which may arise from the Persons disaffected to the State." The law required an oath of allegiance to the state from all residents, and detailed activities that would be considered treasonous.

April 15, 1777

Brig. Gen. James Moore of North Carolina died of gout. He was replaced as commander of the Southern Department of the Continental Army by Brigadier General Robert Howe, also of North Carolina.

April 25–28, 1777

Former North Carolina royal governor and current New York governor William Tryon, now also a major general of provincial forces in the British Army, raided Connecticut. Landing on April 25, his force consisted of British soldiers and Loyalists under the operational command of Brig. Gens. Sir William Erskine and James Agnew. They seized Danbury and destroyed supplies there. Continental Army officers Maj. Gen. David Wooster and Brig. Gens. Gold Silliman and Benedict Arnold were hampered by the lack of available regular forces and had to rely on militia. The British defeated the Patriots at Ridgefield on April 27 and re-embarked the next day. Although the raid was successful, it solidified support for the Patriot cause in the state.

May 27, 1777

Leaders of the Cherokee Nation signed the Treaty of DeWitt's Corner in South Carolina with representatives from both Carolinas, Virginia, and Georgia. The terms included large land concessions on the part of the Cherokee to the state authorities.

The General Assembly met at Tryon Palace, beginning in 1770 and throughout much of the Revolutionary and post-Revolutionary eras. Illustration by Stephen Marchesi.

June 14–October 17, 1777

The Saratoga Campaign. Sir William Howe's strategy for 1777 was to advance on Philadelphia, seat of the Continental government, and on the portion of the Continental Army under Washington's direct command. Separate plans made by Lt. Gen. John Burgoyne were approved by the British government for a campaign to be launched from Quebec. Lord George Germain allowed the generals to plan things on their own, and there was no coordination between the different campaigns, with the result that Burgoyne was not militarily supported by Howe. Burgoyne suffered delays and setbacks in his advance. In September and October Burgoyne fought two major battles with a Patriot army commanded by Maj. Gen. Horation Gates in the general area of Saratoga, New York. The first was a pyrrhic victory for the British, while the second was a Patriot victory. Burgoyne was subsequently forced to surrender. The loss of Burgoyne's army was a major boost to Patriot morale at a time when the occupation of Philadelphia and successive defeats of Washington's army cast doubts on the future of the rebellion, and played a major role in the French decision to openly ally itself with the Continental government in the following year.

June 14–23, 1777

Burgoyne's campaign was essentially a larger and more elaborate version of Sir Guy Carleton's plan from the previous year. Two columns under Burgoyne's overall command would advance southward from Quebec Province, unite in Albany, New York, and move via the Hudson River Valley toward New York City with the object of cutting off the New England states. The campaign began on June 14 when the column under Burgoyne's direct command moved south from St.-Jean-sur-Richelieu toward Lake Champlain. Burgoyne's second, smaller column, under Bvt. Brig. Gen. Barry St. Leger, left the vicinity of Montreal on June 23. Burgoyne's plan was for St. Leger to advance via Lake Ontario to Fort Oswego, New York, and then move eastward to the Mohawk River, to unite with Burgoyne at Albany (Saratoga Campaign).

June 30–July 6, 1777

Burgoyne occupied Crown Point on June 30, and besieged Fort Ticonderoga beginning on July 2. The garrison withdrew on July 6 (Saratoga Campaign).

July 20, 1777

The Treaty of Fort Henry was signed between representatives of the Cherokee Nation and the governments of Virginia and North Carolina at modern-day Kingsport, Tennessee. The treaty provided for the establishment of a garrison on the Chota River, in Cherokee territory, that would be commanded by James Robertson, Superintendent of Indian Affairs for North Carolina. A large group of Cherokee under the leadership of Dragging Canoe refused to abide by the terms of either the Fort Henry or DeWitt's Corner treaties. Removing farther west, they settled on Chickamauga Creek near modern-day Chattanooga, Tennessee. They were referred to by the settlers as the Chickamauga Cherokee and continued to conduct raids on settlers in the western backcountry.

July 23, 1777–July 6, 1778

The Philadelphia Campaign. Sir William Howe transported his army by sea from New York City to Chesapeake Bay, captured the Patriot capital of Philadelphia, and defeated George Washington's army in a series of battles, yet failed to destroy it. Washington's army entered winter quarters at Valley Forge, Pennsylvania, in December and endured a harsh

Cherokee Warriors. Many Cherokee refused to submit to the colonists and moved further west, where they continued their resistance against White encroachment on their lands. Illustration by Stephen Marchesi.

winter but also received valuable military training. Feeling unsupported by the Cabinet in London, Howe resigned as commander-in-chief in October 1777 and was replaced by Sir Henry Clinton in the spring of 1778. Clinton was immediately burdened with a major change in British strategy, the result of France's entry into the war on the side of the United States. He was ordered to detach significant numbers of his troops to other areas, abandon Philadelphia, and return to New York, which he carried out in June.

July 23, 1777

Sir William Howe and a force of some 15,000 men set sail on transports from New York City for Philadelphia on this date, escorted by warships under the command of his brother, Adm. Sir Richard Howe. Washington was initially unsure of how to react, as it was unclear where the British were heading. He was also uncertain as to whether or not Burgyone's advance was merely a feint to draw him off from the protection of Philadelphia (Philadelphia Campaign).

August 2–22, 1777

Siege of Fort Stanwix, New York. Bvt. Brig. Gen. Barry St. Leger's force besieged this key fortification as he advanced toward Albany to link up with Burgoyne. Most of his Indian allies abandoned him during the siege, which was raised on the approach of a Patriot relief force. St. Leger withdrew and attempted to join Burgoyne by way of Lake Champlain but was unable to unite with him. The failure of St. Leger's column to join Burgoyne played a key role in the latter's eventual defeat (Saratoga Campaign).

August 4, 1777

Maj. Gen. Horatio Gates was selected by Congress to replace Maj. Gen. Philip Schyler as commander of the Northern Department of the Continental Army, partly due to the public and political outcry following the fall of Fort Ticonderoga in July. Gates assumed command on August 19 (Saratoga Campaign).

August 5, 1777

The fleet carrying Sir William Howe's army from New York City finally entered Chesapeake Bay after a series of weather-related delays. Upon hearing the news, Washington moved his forces to protect the national capital (Philadelphia Campaign).

August 16, 1777

Battle of Bennington (fought in New York but named after a nearby town in Vermont). A force was detached by Burgoyne on August 9 to raid the Bennington area for supplies. On August 16, they were stopped ten miles short of their goal by a larger force of Patriot militia, defeated, and most of its members captured. The battle resulted in a significant loss of manpower for Burgoyne's army and the subsequent loss of his Indian allies, who lost confidence in his leadership (Saratoga Campaign).

August 25, 1777

Sir William Howe began landing his army at the northern end of Chesapeake Bay in Maryland (Philadelphia Campaign).

September 11, 1777

Battle of Brandywine, Pennsylvania. Washington's efforts to block Sir William Howe's advance failed when he was defeated (Philadelphia Campaign).

September 19, 1777

Battle of Freeman's Farm (First Battle of Saratoga). By early September Burgoyne had learned of St. Leger's failure at Fort Stanwix and that he would receive no real support from Howe. Faced with the dilemma of continuing to advance on Albany or to turn back to Fort Ticonderoga, he decided on Albany. In mid-September, he crossed the Hudson River and headed south. On September 19, he he attempted to outflank the left of Gates's defensive works and was met by a reconnaissance-in-force under Daniel Morgan, who was reinforced as the fighting intensified. Burgoyne won a Pyrrhic victory, gaining the field at the cost of high casualties (Saratoga Campaign).

September 25, 1777

Philadelphia was captured by Sir William Howe. Congress fled beforehand and soon established a new capital in York, Pennsylvania (Philadelphia Campaign).

October 3–26, 1777

A raid up the Hudson River from New York City was launched by Sir Henry Clinton as a diversionary effort to cause Gates to abandon his position in front of Burgoyne. Although the raid achieved some success, capturing two Patriot forts on the river on October 6, it did not go far enough north to link up with Burgoyne or to cause Gates to abandon his position (Saratoga Campaign).

October 4, 1777

Battle of Germantown, Pennsylvania. Washington attacked a strong British force of 9,000 at this location and was repulsed. During the battle, the initial Patriot attack was successful but soon broke down in confusion due to a heavy fog. The British and Hessian troops counterattacked and drove the Americans back. The North Carolina Brigade, under Brig. Gen. Francis Nash, was in reserve, but was brought forward late in the day to cover the Patriot retreat. During the subsequent fighting, Nash was mortally wounded and died on October 7. Nash County and its county seat of Nashville are named for him (Philadelphia Campaign).

October 7, 1777

Battle of Bemis Heights (Second Battle of Saratoga). Burgoyne ordered a reconnaissance of the Patriot left flank and was met by a large force sent by Gates to counter his movement. The British were driven back to their camp. Outnumbered, Burgoyne withdrew northward the following day (Saratoga Campaign).

October 17, 1777

Surrounded by Gates's army, Burgoyne's army surrendered at Saratoga. The surrender was the most important Patriot victory in the Revolutionary War to date with the surrender of nearly 6,000 British and Hessian troops, a significant loss of manpower for the British. The surrender raised Patriot morale following the defeats suffered in the Philadelphia campaign. Negotiations between United States representatives and the French government began two days after the arrival of the news of Saratoga in Paris, resulting in the Franco-American alliance the following year. The tide was slowly beginning to turn against the British, and their continued failure to achieve victory in the North and mid-Atlantic led many British policymakers to argue that military operations should shift southward, with the idea of regaining the Southern colonies, leaving for later the option of a possible subsequent reconquest of the North or, alternatively, an independent America smaller in size, economically weak, and easily dominated by a British empire controlling the South, the trans-Appalachian, and Quebec Province.

November 15, 1777

The Continental Congress finalized the Articles of Confederation and Perpetual Union, the original system of government for the United States. It codified the various laws passed by Congress into a single system. As a reaction to the conflicts with the British Crown and Parliament that led to the Revolution, the Articles established a weak national government made up of a confederation of thirteen sovereign states. Congress functioned as the national governing body. The weakness of the confederation government gradually became apparent. In the meantime, the Articles went to the states for ratification in a process that took four years to complete.

December 19, 1777–June 19, 1778

The Continental Army was in winter quarters at Valley Forge, Pennsylvania, where the troops suffered through a rough winter, plagued by supply problems. A fresh outbreak of smallpox in the ranks, due to somewhere between 3,000 and 4,000 men on the rolls not being inoculated according to orders, caused Washington to order a second enforced inoculation of the troops in January 1778. Other diseases such as typhus plagued the army. Besides starvation and disease, the size of the army greatly diminished due to desertion and enlistment expirations. Many of the issues that the army faced were addressed in a reorganization authorized by Congress on May 27, 1778. It included disbanding some units and the incorporation of the remaining soldiers into other units. Besides this much-needed reorganization, the troops were trained by Prussian military officer Baron Friedrich Wilhelm von Steuben (Philadelphia Campaign).

February 6, 1778

In Paris, representatives for the United States and France signed the Treaty of Amity and Commerce, which brought formal French recognition of American independence and established economic relations between the two nations. They also signed the Treaty of Alliance, a defensive pact.

March 8, 1778

Lord George Germain wrote Gen. Sir Henry Clinton of George III's desire for the conquest of the Southern colonies. Germain was one of many British political or military figures convinced that the South's Loyalist population was greater than it was (although it was stronger there than in other parts of the colonies), and that a major British show of force was all that was needed to prompt their flocking to the British standard. In addition, he believed the loss of the Southern colonies would be a major economic blow to the United States. This marked a shift in British military planning to a Southern strategy for winning the war. Germain left the details of the planning for any subsequent campaign to Clinton, who had been designated to succeed Howe. Howe resigned in October 1777 but still awaited formal confirmation that his resignation had been accepted.

March 13, 1778

The French government formally notified Great Britain of their full recognition of the United States as an independent nation and the existence of the Treaty of Amity and Commerce and the Treaty of Alliance. Although there was no formal declaration of war by either nation, the revelation of a military alliance between France and the United States was a de facto announcement that France was at war with Britain, and both nations began preparations for a conflict. Britain was soon faced with hard choices regarding how much of its military resources could be devoted to the subjugation of America, and how much had to be used against the French, especially as George III and other members of the British government very quickly thought of possible gains for the British empire at France's expense, particularly in the West Indies.

March 21, 1778

With the outbreak of hostilities with France, Germain ordered Clinton to abandon Philadelphia and retreat to New York, as well as send 3,000 troops to East Florida and 5,000 troops to the West Indies. Upon receipt of the instructions in April, Clinton dispatched the troops to East Florida but declined to send men to the West Indies until November, due to a lack of transports. From that point on, the British had difficulty getting reinforcements sent to America, affecting the outcome of future campaigns.

April 14–May 2, 1778

The North Carolina General Assembly met in New Bern. It reelected Caswell as governor and appointed three members to the Continental Congress: Cornelius Harnett, John Penn, and John Williams (Abner Nash was initially selected, but refused to take the position, and Williams went in his stead). The legislature also organized more Continental troops and militia, as well as supplies and other military necessities.

North Carolina militiamen in their encampment. Illustration by Stephen Marchesi.

April 24, 1778

Both houses of the North Carolina General Assembly confirmed a resolution authorizing North Carolina's delegates to the Continental Congress to vote for ratification of the Articles of Confederation.

May 24, 1778

Sir Henry Clinton replaced Sir William Howe as commander-in-chief of the British forces in America. Howe had resigned in October 1777, claiming that he lacked support from the government during the Philadelphia Campaign. Acceptance of his resignation was received in April 1778. Howe sailed for England on May 25.

May 29, 1778

On May 27, the Continental Congress authorized a reorganization of the Continental Army to address many of the issues plaguing the Army during the winter encampment at Valley Forge, including losses due to starvation, disease, desertion, and enlistment expirations. The reorganization included the disbanding of some units and the incorporation of the remaining soldiers into other units. The new organization set the size of "battalions" (regiments) at nine full strength companies. On May 29, Congress turned its attention specifically to the North Carolina units and ordered that those regiments in camp at Valley Forge be reorganized according to the new system. Excess officers were sent home to North Carolina, where they were assigned to four new regiments (beyond those at Valley Forge), and only four, which for the present would be on duty in the state. Any excess officers beyond these reorganizations were dismissed from the service. The understrength size of the regiments of the North Carolina Continental Line prompted these changes. As a result, the men and officers of the 6th Regiment were consolidated into the 1st, those of the 4th were consolidated into the 2nd, while those of the 5th were consolidated into the 3rd. The 7th, 8th, and 9th Regiments and the newly arrived 10th Regiment were disbanded and their officers and men distributed among the three remaining regiments. The leftover officers were sent back to North Carolina to begin recruiting the four new regiments authorized by Congress, which if completed would carry the numerical designations of the old 4th, 5th, 6th and 7th Regiments.

June–July 1778

Loyalist militia officers and raiders Samuel Smith and David Fanning were captured at Gilbert Town, North Carolina, sometime during June, and taken as prisoners to Ninety-Six in South Carolina. Fanning escaped shortly after his arrival, was recaptured, and escaped again. Upon returning to North Carolina, he joined up with a Loyalist militia force under the command of Col. Ambrose Mills that was recruiting men for an expedition into East Florida. One of the recruits was a Patriot spy whose information led to the capture of Mills and sixteen of his men. Fanning and fourteen men pursued the Patriot cavalry and their captives, skirmishing with them near Salisbury. The outcome was inconclusive. Shortly afterward, Fanning was captured and sent to Ninety-Six once again, but soon afterward escaped another time. Thus began a cycle of recaptures and fresh escapes that lasted through the year. During one of his brief periods of freedom, Fanning recruited more men to the Loyalist cause before he was recaptured near Salisbury sometime in July. He was soon on the loose again.

June–November 1778

Now that Britain was at war with France, the British government sought to end the conflict with the colonists but, unrealistically, without granting them independence. The Carlisle Peace Commission, headed by Frederick Howard, 5th Earl of Carlisle, was sent to America. On June 13, as Clinton prepared to evacuate Philadelphia, the commission sent a series of proposals to the Continental Congress that the British hoped would lead to reconciliation. Congress immediately placed two preconditions on any negotiations, recognition of American independence and the complete withdrawal of all British forces, which the commission lacked the authorization to grant. The commissioners tried various tactics to bring the Continental government to the negotiation table, including statements issued to the general public of the devastation that would incur if the war continued, but nothing succeeded. In November, the commissioners returned to Britain.

June 28, 1778–February 25, 1779

The Northwestern Campaign (also known as the Illinois Campaign). A series of campaigns waged by Lt. Col. George Rogers Clark, who led a small command of Virginia militiamen across the Ohio River into the Illinois Country, comprised of lands that today make up much of the modern-day states of Illinois and Indiana. The territory had been ceded by France to Britain at the end of the Seven Years' War. Clark in quick succession captured Kaskaskia, Cahokia, and Vincennes. Many of the White settlers in the region were French and cooperated with the invaders against the British. Henry Hamilton, Lieutenant Governor and Superintendent of Indian Affairs for the Illinois Country, retook Vincennes on December 17. Clark and a small command, almost half of which came from the French population of the region, successfully besieged Vincennes on February 23–25, after an overland march of 180 miles from Kaskaskia. Virginia subsequently claimed the Illinois Country, but ceded it to the national government in 1781, after which it was combined with other land ceded to the United States at the end of the war and became the Northwest Territory.

June 28, 1778

The Battle of Monmouth Court House, New Jersey. Ordered by Lord Germain to abandon Philadelphia, Clinton's army marched to New York City beginning on June 15. En route, the British were attacked by the Continental Army on this date. The bloody see-saw fight that followed was inconclusive, although it showed that the Continental Army was finally a match for the British regulars due to von Steuben's training.

July–August 1778

The General Assembly met again. It sent two more delegates to the Continental Congress, Whitmell Hill and Thomas Burke.

July 11–22, 1778

Five days after the last of Clinton's troops were carried to New York by transports, a French squadron arrived off Sandy Hook, New Jersey, the southern end of the entrance to New York Harbor. Commanded by Adm. Charles Henri Hector, Comte d'Estaing, the squadron of sixteen warships blockaded the harbor and Admiral Lord Howe's smaller fleet for eleven days. As d'Estaing's largest ships drew too much water to cross the bar into the harbor itself, it was decided by d'Estaing and his American allies that he should sail north and cooperate with American forces recapturing Newport, Rhode Island. However, while d'Estaing still blockaded the harbor mouth, Clinton bypassed him and sent 2,000 troops through Long Island Sound by troop transport to reinforce the British garrison at Newport.

July 21, 1778

North Carolina's delegates to the Continental Congress ratified the Articles of Confederation.

July 27, 1778

The Battle of Ushant, an inconclusive naval clash between British and French fleets near the opening into the English Channel, was fought on this date. It was the first battle between the old rivals since the declarations of war in March.

August 21-October 19, 1778

Siege of Pondicherry (modern Puducherry), India. An army of 10,500 British and British East India Company soldiers under Gen. Sir Hector Munro, supported by a squadron under Adm. Edward Vernon (for whom Washington's Mount Vernon was named, as Washington's older half-brother Lawrence Washington served under Vernon in the War of Jenkins' Ear), successfully besieged the capital of France's India colony, defended by 1,100 French and colonial Indian troops under Gov. and Gen. Guillaume de Bellecombe. The fall of the city to the British marked the beginning of a series of British conquests of French posts in India which eventually led to a confederation of France's Indian allies launching an invasion of British territory in the outbreak of the Second Mysore War in July 1780, as Britain's imperial ambitions slowly dragged it into an international military situation that was way over its head.

August 24, 1778

A return of Black men serving in the Continental Army, then at White Plains, New York, was compiled. It showed fifty-eight Black men serving in the regiments of the North Carolina Continental Line, interspersed among the White soldiers. At least 468 Black men from North Carolina are known to have fought for or supported the Revolutionary War, including those who served in state militia units.

August 29, 1778

Battle of Newport, Rhode Island. An American force, supported by d'Estaing's French squadron, attempted to recapture this important port. Just before the battle, a powerful storm, possibly a hurricane, dispersed d'Estaing's force. Instead of continuing the battle, the French sailed

A Black Continental Soldier. Black soldiers served among their White comrades in the North Carolina Continental Line. Illustration by Stephen Marchesi.

to Boston to regroup and refit, as they were in dire need of supplies after crossing the Atlantic. Having lost its French naval support, the Continental forces attempted to capture the town on their own, but their siege failed and they decided to withdraw in the face of news that Clinton had dispatched reinforcements by sea from New York City. Though unsuccessful, the campaign marked the first direct cooperation in the war between American and French forces.

September 7, 1778

The French seized the Caribbean island of Dominica, a former possession lost to Britain in 1761. The island is located between the islands of Martinique and Guadeloupe, then both French-controlled islands. The British government was surprised by the attack, and preparations were quickly made to launch a counteroffensive in the Caribbean.

September 25, 1778

The Continental Congress appointed Maj. Gen. Benjamin Lincoln of Massachusetts, a veteran officer who had served under Washington and also under Gates in the Saratoga Campaign, to replace North Carolina's Maj. Gen. Robert Howe. Howe had long been the subject of criticism due to his difficult working relationships with the Patriot governors of South Carolina and Georgia, his August 1778 duel with prominent South Carolina politician Christopher Gadsen, and his reputation for forming controversial relationships with women other than his wife. Howe remained acting commander of the department until Lincoln's arrival.

November 3, 1778

A British squadron under Commodore William Hofham departed from Sandy Hook on this date, escorting transports carrying 5,000 British troops under Maj. Gen. James Grant. Their intended targets were French colonial possessions in the West Indies. The movement illustrates how the addition of France to the war rapidly widened the scope and war aims of the conflict, while further diminishing the available number of troops in North America for Clinton to utilize in direct military operations against the Patriots. On the same day, d'Estaing sailed from Boston, with the West Indies also his destination.

December 13–28, 1778

The St. Lucia campaign. Hofham arrived in the West Indies first, as d'Estaing's fleet was scattered in a storm and had to regroup. Hofham united with the British Leeward Islands fleet under Adm. Samuel Barrington on December 10. Their intended target was the French-occupied island of St. Lucia. The campaign was a British success. St. Lucia served as a major base for the British in the region for the remainder of the war.

December 29, 1778

A British joint army-navy expedition under Lt. Col. Archibald Campbell and Commodore Hyde Parker captured Savannah, Georgia, as the British Southern strategy swung into operation. The Americans, under Maj. Gen. Robert Howe of North Carolina, were badly routed and suffered heavy losses in both killed and captured. Howe was subsequently criticized for his troop dispositions and for even attempting to defend the city instead of safely withdrawing his troops and keeping them intact until reinforced by Lincoln.

January 3, 1779

Maj. Gen. Benjamin Lincoln and 1,500 men arrived at Purrysburg, South Carolina, on the Georgia border, and united with Maj. Gen. Robert Howe and the remnants of his force from Savannah. Lincoln assumed formal command of the Southern Department of the Continental Army.

January 17, 1779

Maj. Gen. Augustine Prevost, commander of British forces in East Florida, arrived in Savannah to assume command of British forces in Georgia from Lt. Col. Archibald Campbell.

January 19–February 13, 1779

The North Carolina General Assembly went into session. It formed eight new counties: Franklin, Gates, Jones, Lincoln, Montgomery, Randolph, Rutherford, and Warren. John Williams resigned from the Continental Congress, and the legislature sent two new delegates, Joseph Hewes and William Sharpe.

January 29, 1779

A British expedition from Savannah under Lt. Col. Archibald Campbell occupied Augusta, Georgia, as part of a campaign to restore the Georgia backcountry to British control. Campbell's attempt to recruit Loyalists in the region, with the intent of raising a force large enough to march on Charleston, was not very successful, underscoring the problem that British supporters of a Southern strategy faced in regard to the realities of the level of actual Loyalist support in the region. Campbell's force was closely monitored by Brig. Gen. Andrew Williamson, commanding South Carolina and Georgia militia and encamped across the Savannah River from Augusta.

February 3, 1779

Battle of Beaufort, South Carolina. On January 29, 1779, Maj. Gen. Prevost dispatched a force of nearly 200 men drawn from two British infantry regiments under Maj. William Gardner by sea to Port Royal Island, South Carolina, an area rumored to be dominated by Loyalists. Gardner's immediate task was to act as a distraction from Campbell's expedition to Augusta, but it was also intended to establish a base for the recruitment of Loyalists and prepare for a larger British invasion of South Carolina later in the year. Gardner's force landed on the island on February 2. Meanwhile, Benjamin Lincoln became aware of Gardner's expedition and sent a force of 300 South Carolina militiamen under Brig. Gen. William Moultrie to Port Royal Island. Moultrie landed on February 1 and occupied Beaufort. On February 3, the two forces clashed in a brief but intense fight in which Gardner's men were repulsed and lost nearly a fifth of its strength killed or captured. Gardner withdrew from the island without receiving any Loyalist support, and Lincoln was not distracted from Campbell's operations in Georgia.

February 14, 1779

Campbell withdrew from Augusta after receiving news that Williamson had been reinforced by a large force of North Carolina militia under Maj. Gen. John Ashe. Williamson reoccupied Augusta, while Ashe followed Campbell as he moved toward Savannah.

February 14, 1779

Battle of Kettle Creek, Georgia. Upon departing Savannah on January 24 in his drive to capture Augusta, Lt. Col. Archibald Campbell had dispatched Lt. Col. John Boyd to recruit Loyalists in the Carolina backcountry. Boyd traveled to Anson County, North Carolina, where he quickly recruited hundreds of men among local Scottish settlers, many of whom had served in the Moores Creek Campaign. Turning south, Boyd and his recruits marched toward Augusta through South Carolina, adding more recruits while plundering the countryside. Col. Andrew Pickens and a force of about 350 South Carolina militia moved to intercept Boyd, whose men numbered between 600 and 800 by the time they encamped at Kettle Creek, a tributary of the Savannah River. Although seriously outnumbered, Pickens attacked and surprised Boyd's camp, scattering the Loyalists after a brief but difficult fight and mortally wounding Boyd.

March 3, 1779

Battle of Briar Creek, Georgia. Following his abandonment of Augusta, Lt. Col. Archibald Campbell withdrew along the Savannah River in the direction of Savannah, halting at Ebenezer, Georgia. There he turned over command of his force to Lt. Col. Jacques Marcus "Mark" Prevost, younger brother of Brigadier General Prevost, appointed him lieutenant governor of Georgia, and returned to England. Campbell also outlined a plan for Prevost to attack a pursuing Patriot force under the command of Maj. Gen. John Ashe of North Carolina. Ashe encamped on Briar Creek, a tributary of the Savannah, on February 27, and began repairing a bridge across the creek. His force consisted of North Carolina militia, reinforced in camp by a regiment of Georgia Continentals under Col. Samuel Elbert and some light cavalry, bolstering his numbers to nearly 1,300. Prevost carried out Campbell's plan on March 3, marching nearly 1,000 men around the Patriots and launching a surprise attack from the north. The militia were routed, and while Elbert's Continentals put up a stiff fight they were surrounded and mostly captured. The British victory provided a check on the Patriot resurgence in the Georgia backcountry. Ashe was later court-martialed for negligence to properly protect the camp and for cowardice. He was cleared of the latter charge but found guilty of having failed to provide security for the camp.

April–Fall 1779

Smallpox outbreaks afflicted parts of North Carolina. In New Bern, a serious outbreak forced the General Assembly to cancel its plans to meet. Meanwhile, elements of Pulaski's Legion passing through Salem introduced smallpox to the Moravian community. Nearly thirty percent of the village's inhabitants contracted the disease, although only three people died.

April 12, 1779

The French and Spanish signed the Treaty of Aranjuez, which brought Spain into France's war against Britain in return for France's help in recovering territories lost by Spain to Britain in previous conflicts. Significantly, Spain would not ally itself with the United States, partly over worries that the revolution might prove to be an unfortunate inspiration to Spain's own American colonies. The Spanish thus only participated in campaigns outside of United States territory and that were directed to regaining lost territorial possessions. Spain did, however, continue to send military supplies to the new nation.

April 23, 1779

Benjamin Lincoln marched from Purrysburg, South Carolina with the bulk of his army toward Augusta, Georgia, with a somewhat nebulous plan to suppress Loyalist unrest in the Georgia backcountry. Augusta was already occupied by the South Carolina militia of Andrew Williamson, however, and in marching toward Augusta, Lincoln left South Carolina virtually undefended except for Moultrie and about 1,000 militiamen and slightly over 200 Continentals. Moultrie was ordered by Lincoln to concentrate at Purrysburg and to delay any British advance on Charleston, which Lincoln thought very unlikely, until Lincoln returned and joined him.

April 29, 1779

Facing supply problems and somewhat taken aback by Lincoln's move toward Augusta, Augustine Prevost in Savannah decided to take advantage of the departure of the majority of the Patriot army and invade South Carolina. On this date he crossed the Savannah, attacked Moultrie's force at Purrysburg, and drove it back. The Patriots were rescued from total disaster by the Savannah River itself, swollen from recent rains, which slowed Prevost for two days in getting his artillery and supplies across.

Moultrie fell back to the Coosawatchie River to regroup and began sending a series of messages to Lincoln to return to his aid or at least detach part of his force to return to South Carolina, while Lincoln downplayed the threat until well into early May.

May 3–May 15, 1779

The General Assembly met in Smithfield, due to the smallpox outbreak in New Bern. Richard Caswell was reelected governor, while John Penn and Cornelius Harnett were reelected as delegates to the Continental Congress.

May 11–12, 1779

Battle of Charleston, South Carolina. Moultrie withdrew backward toward Charleston as Prevost continued to advance. The Patriot commander lost much of his force on the way, as many of the South Carolina militiamen left to defend their homes and families. The remainder, about 600 men, reached Charleston where they were reinforced by Polish exile Brig. Gen. Count Casimir Pulaski's Legion from Washington's army. Other reinforcements, including additional South Carolina militiamen and Benjamin Lincoln's army, at last on the move from Georgia, marched toward Charleston. Prevost's forces seized the ferry across the Ashley River on May 10, where Moultrie had carelessly failed to gather up the boats tethered there. Prevost used them to cross part of his force and sealed off Charleston Neck. The British lacked the numbers to take the city by storm, and after two days of skirmishing withdrew to James Island on the night of May 12–13 after receiving word of the approach of Lincoln's army.

June 9–July 5, 1779

The French launched a naval campaign against British possessions in the West Indies. Saint Vincent, south of St. Lucia, was captured in a short campaign waged June 16–18. Meanwhile, d'Estaing captured Grenada on July 5.

June 20, 1779

Battle of Stono Ferry, South Carolina. Following his withdrawal from Charleston, Prevost planned to retreat back into Georgia via South Carolina's coastal islands. His withdrawal was somewhat leisurely, and his troops spent much time foraging and plundering the countryside.

Attempts to recruit large numbers of Loyalists failed, an increasingly familiar scenario for the British in the South. By the beginning of June, he had withdrawn from James Island to Johns Island, with the exception of a well-defended bridgehead on the mainland at the ferry on the Stono River. Benjamin Lincoln decided to attack the bridgehead when he received word that the British were withdrawing as Prevost prepared to retreat into Georgia. The British defensive line held until the approach of reinforcements from Prevost, prompting Lincoln to withdraw. Prevost resumed his retreat to Savannah, which he reached in mid-July.

June 24, 1779–February 7, 1783

The Siege of Gibraltar by the Spanish and the French. Gibraltar guarded the gateway from the Atlantic into the Mediterranean Sea. Britain shifted many of its military and naval resources away from America to keep this important post operating and eventually relieved.

June 30, 1779

Gen. Sir Henry Clinton issued what became known as the Philipsburg Proclamation, which proclaimed the freedom of all enslaved people belonging to Patriot owners, regardless of whether or not they were willing to fight for the British.

July 25–September 3, 1779

The Armada of 1779, a massive fleet of thirty French and thirty-six Spanish ships of the line, supported by many smaller warships and commanded by the French Adm. Louis Guillouet, Comte d'Orvilliers, set sail from northwestern Spain for the English Channel in late July. The plan was to escort an army of over 40,000 French soldiers from ports in northern France to invade England after establishing a base on the Channel Islands. The fleet sailed into the channel unopposed in mid-August, as the British Channel Fleet was patrolling farther west after having received word that the French contingent of the armada had set sail in June. The armada arrived off of Plymouth and set off a huge panic in Britain, which had few regular troops available on the home islands for a defense. Before the Allied Fleet could begin escorting the troop transports from the French ports to England, d'Orvilliers received orders from the French government to backtrack and sail westward, with the idea of landing the troops in Cornwall. D'Orvilliers protested the change of plans, and while waiting for clarification, the armada remained off of Plymouth, where it was struck by a gale, blown westward into the Atlantic, and partly scattered. The Channel Fleet, meanwhile, received word of the armada and headed eastward. The two fleets missed contact with each other on a foggy night, and the British fleet reached the strait separating Southampton and Portsmouth from the Isle of Wight and prepared to fight. D'Orvilliers decided to abandon the campaign, however, as the ships' crews suffered from sickness and diminishing supplies. Although no troops actually left France, the threat of an invasion illustrated vividly the strain that the widening war had on Britain's military resources.

August 27, 1779–May 10, 1781

The Mississippi Valley and Gulf Coast Campaign was launched by Bernardo de Gálvez, governor of Spanish Louisiana, to recapture territory that Spain lost to Britain in the Seven Years' War. This was the old Spanish province of Florida, divided by the British into the colonies of East Florida (the bulk of modern-day Florida, with a capital at St. Augustine) and West Florida (modern-day Florida west of the Apalachicola River and the Gulf Coast portions of modern-day Alabama, Mississippi, and Louisiana east of the Mississippi River, with a capital at Pensacola). The British surrendered all of British West Florida on May 10, 1781, after Gálvez captured all of the important British posts along the Gulf Coast, including Pensacola. The campaign not only cost the British a colonial possession but siphoned off troops and naval vessels that could otherwise have been used for suppressing the Revolution.

September 7, 1779

Spanish capture of Fort Bute (Battle of Manchac Post), in southeastern Louisiana. Bernardo de Gálvez opened his campaign against the British in West Florida after receiving word of the Spanish declaration of war and intercepting a message that the British planned to attack New Orleans. Opting to strike the British first, he attacked and captured this run-down stockade built during the Seven Years'/French and Indian War, defended by twenty German grenadiers (Mississippi Valley and Gulf Coast Campaign).

September 12–21, 1779

Siege of Fort New Richmond (Baton Rouge), Louisiana. Advancing from Fort Bute, Gálvez and a force numbering perhaps 800 Spanish regulars and Acadian militiamen besieged Baton Rouge, garrisoned by about 400 British regulars and German grenadiers as well as artillery.

After a heavy bombardment on September 21, British commander Lt. Col. Alexander Dickson surrendered not only the fort but all other British posts on the Mississippi River. After garrisoning the fort, Gálvez returned to New Orleans and began planning a campaign to take Mobile and Pensacola (Mississippi Valley and Gulf Coast Campaign).

September 19–October 16, 1779

The Americans and French attempted to retake Savannah. The Southern Department of the Continental Army was commanded by Maj. Gen. Benjamin Lincoln; French troops and the French naval squadron were commanded by Admiral d'Estaing and included a regiment of Black men from Sainte-Domingue (the future Haiti). The British defenders were commanded by Gen. Augustine Prevost. The allied forces laid siege beginning September 19. From October 3 to October 8, the French naval squadron conducted a massive bombardment of the city's defenses, which failed to reduce them. This led to d'Estaing deciding on a land assault, which occurred on October 9. It was a disastrous failure, with the allies suffering heavy casualties. As a result, they abandoned the siege on October 16.

September 23, 1779

On this date, what was probably the most famous naval engagement of the war (although hardly the largest or most important) occurred off of Flamborough Head on the coast of Yorkshire, England. Scottish-born American privateer John Paul Jones attacked a convoy of forty-one British merchant vessels guarded by the British frigate *Serapis* and the sloop *Countess of Scarborough*. Jones's squadron consisted of his own vessel, the *Bonhomme Richard*, a former merchant ship converted into a warship, the American frigate *Alliance*, the French brig *Vengeance*, and the French frigate *Pallas*. Jones was victorious, capturing the *Serapis*, although the *Bonhomme Richard* was so badly damaged that it sank two days later. Although the *Pallas* captured the *Countess of Scarborough*, the *Alliance* and the *Vengeance* contributed little to the fight. The victory was the most famous of Jones' distinguished career as a privateer who preyed on British merchant vessels in the waters of the British Isles.

October 18–November 10, 1779

The General Assembly met in Halifax. It formed three new counties: Richmond, Sullivan (now in Tennessee), and Wayne. Delegates to the

Continental Congress for the year 1780 were John Penn, Cornelius Harnett, William Sharpe, Thomas Burke, Whitmell Hill, and Allen Jones.

October 25, 1779

The British evacuated Rhode Island, and the 6,000 troops stationed there joined Clinton's main army in and around New York City. Clinton and Adm. Mariot Arbuthnot became concerned during the fall when they received reports that d'Estaing was sailing northward from the West Indies. Unsure of his target, it was decided best to consolidate the British forces in Rhode Island with those in New York City, as the events of the 1778 campaign had revealed that Rhode Island was hard to defend. As it turned out, d'Estaing's target was Savannah and his operation had already failed. The addition of the Rhode Island garrison factored into Clinton's planning for a campaign in South Carolina, as it made more British troops available for the operation.

December 26, 1779

Clinton sailed from New York with a fleet of fourteen warships and ninety troopships, the latter carrying 8,500 soldiers, to reinforce British forces in the South and launch the reconquest of South Carolina, beginning with Charleston. Cornwallis was his second-in-command. Bad weather scattered the fleet, and the bulk of it did not reassemble until the period of January 24–February 1, 1780, when it reached the mouth of the Savannah River on the latter date.

February 11–12, 1780

Clinton's troops landed unopposed on Wadmalaw Island (Simmons/Seabrook Island in many sources), thirty miles south of Charleston. On February 14, they began to march toward Stono Ferry, from which they could cross to James Island in Charleston Harbor.

February 25, 1780

Clinton's troops crossed onto James Island at Stono Ferry. Throughout the remainder of February, and all of March, they gradually gained control of the island's fortifications. They reached the Ashley River and the southern part of Charleston Harbor, and moved onto the mainland with the goal of cutting off the city from the landward side.

March 2–14, 1780

Siege of Mobile (Fort Charlotte), West Florida (modern Alabama). Gálvez left New Orleans on January 28 and sailed to Mobile Bay, which he reached on February 9. Receiving reinforcements en route and additional reinforcements from Cuba after his arrival, Gálvez landed and proceeded to besiege Fort Charlotte, which guarded the city. The fort was in a run-down state, and its garrison was small, but its commander refused to surrender. After a two-week siege and a heavy bombardment that breached the walls, however, he surrendered. A British relief force from Pensacola failed to arrive in time. The outcome of the siege gave the Spanish control of Mobile Bay. Afterwards, Gálvez returned to New Orleans to plan operations against the better-defended Pensacola (Mississippi Valley and Gulf Coast Campaign).

March 11, 1780

Czarina Catherine II (the Great) of Russia declared her country's neutrality in the ongoing conflict and the right of all European nations to trade with either side as they desired, excepting military matériel. Blockades would not be observed. The declaration would be enforced by the Russian Navy. This led to the creation of the First League of Armed Neutrality in August 1780, when Russia signed an agreement with Denmark-Norway and Sweden. They were subsequently joined over succeeding months by Prussia, Austria, Portugal, the Ottoman Empire, and the Kingdom of Naples. The United States, France, and Spain promised to respect the neutrality of League members. Britain refused to recognize the League, but at the same time declined to interfere with the shipping of League members. Britain's long-time ally and trading partner the Dutch Republic attempted to join, but with unexpected results for the Dutch (see below).

April 1–May 12, 1780

Clinton besieged Charleston, South Carolina. The Americans, commanded by Benjamin Lincoln, were unable to break the siege, and Lincoln and 3,371 men surrendered on May 12. Among those surrendered were the 1st, 2nd, and 3rd North Carolina Regiments of the Continental Line, totaling 814 men, and 1,231 North Carolina militiamen. With Lincoln a prisoner, Johann von Robais, Baron de Kalb, became acting commander of forces in the Southern Department. Even before the siege ended, however, the Continental Congress voted on May 7 to assign command of the department to Gen. Horatio Gates, victor of the Battle of Saratoga.

April 14, 1780

The Battle of Monck's Corner, South Carolin, part of the siege of Charleston. As part of Clinton's plan to completely cut off Charleston from potential reinforcement, he dispatched a force under Col. James Webster to attack Patriots under Brig. Gen. Isaac Huger stationed at Monck's Corner, where they guarded Lincoln's line of communications between Charleston and the outside world. Webster's force consisted of two British infantry regiments, Maj. Patrick Ferguson's Loyalist battalion the American Volunteers, and the British Legion, a Loyalist organization under Lt. Col. Banastre Tarleton, a Briitish officer. Legions were a type of unit popular in the Revolutionary era. Although taking their name from the classical Roman infantry unit, the legions of the Revolutionary era were mixed forces that came into use during the warfare of the 17th century. They were mini-armies, containing infantry, cavalry and artillery units, that operated independently of larger armies or functioned as part of a larger force. Tarleton recruited the Legion in the northern colonies earlier in the war.

Huger's men consisted of a mixture of infantry and cavalry, the latter under Col. William Washington. Tarleton was sent ahead in command of his Legion and Ferguson's Volunteers on the night of April 13 to attack Huger in camp. After intercepting a letter from Huger to Lincoln which describing Huger's deployment, Tarleton pushed on and attacked the camp at 3 a.m. on April 14, routing the Patriots. The battle established Tarleton's reputation as a hard-hitting officer, and the British Legion's for brutality toward Patriots attempting to surrender, and toward local civilians. These accusations resurfaced multiple times during the Carolinas Campaign.

April 17–May 10, 1780

The General Assembly convened in New Bern. As Caswell, by law, could not be governor beyond three terms, Abner Nash was elected as North Carolina's second state governor. Caswell, in turn, was made major general and commandant of all North Carolina militia forces and commanded them at the disaster at Camden on August 16, 1780.

May 22–June 3, 1780

Sir Henry Clinton issued a series of proclamations from Charleston on May 22, June 1, and June 3, 1780, regarding paroles and loyalty. The first proclamation threatened imprisonment and confiscation of property for

Abner Nash, chosen by the North Carolina General Assembly as the state's second governor in April 1780. James Littlejohn Busbee, Abner Nash, 1908–1909, oil on canvas, 30 x 25 in., North Carolina Museum of History, accessed Feb. 26, 2026, https://commons.wikimedia.org/wiki/File:Abner_Nash,_by_James_Littlejohn_Busbee_(1908%E2%80%931909).jpg

anyone who took up arms against the Crown or encouraged others to do so and required that all men join the Loyalist militia. In the second proclamation, he offered a full pardon to all who resubmitted to British rule and took an oath of allegiance, excepting those who had been involved in the execution of Loyalists. Those taking the oath would be recognized fully as citizens and would enjoy freedom from Parliamentary taxation. In the third proclamation, he authorized the release of all paroled Patriots on June 20 but demanded that they sign an oath of allegiance to the monarchy within seventeen days and openly support British efforts to crush the revolution or they would be considered in rebellion. The proclamations ultimately backfired on the British. The second proclamation antagonized Loyalists, who felt that it let repentant Patriots get away with their formerly rebellious activities and allegiance. The third proclamation eliminated the chance for neutrality between former Patriots willing to return to their British allegiance as long as they did not have to take up arms against their former comrades; many thus felt pushed to reject the British terms and return to the fight.

Banastre Tarleton, controversial British officer and commander of the British Legion, a Loyalist force of cavalry, infantry, and artillery recruited primarily in the Northern states. Tarleton gained a reputation for brutality and ruthlessness in the Southern campaign of 1780–1781, but it is often difficult to distinguish the myth from the reality of a man who quickly became a stock villain in Patriot lore. Joshua Reynolds, 1782, Portrait of Sir Banastre Tarleton, oil on canvas, 92.9 x 57 in., National Gallery, London, accessed 26 Feb. 2026, https://commons.wikimedia.org/wiki/File:Banastre-Tarleton-by-Joshua-Reynolds.jpg

May 29, 1780

A skirmish broke out at Waxhaws, South Carolina, between Virginia Continentals and South Carolina militiamen under the command of Col. Abraham Buford, and the British Legion and a contingent of British regulars under the command of Lt. Col. Banastre Tarleton. Buford was escorting a supply train, along with South Carolina's governor and members of his cabinet, in the direction of Hillsborough, North Carolina. Cornwallis, who was consolidating British control of the South Carolina backcountry, sent Tarleton ahead of his main force to intercept them. He caught up with Buford at Waxhaws, although the governor and his officials had already fled the slow-moving Patriot column. Tarleton's cavalry charged and broke Buford's line, routing his men. The Patriots sent out a flag of truce, but as Tarleton rode to it his horse was shot and toppled onto him. His infantrymen, enraged, charged and showed no quarter, bayonetting everyone in sight. Tarleton regained control of the situation once he got disentangled from his dead horse, but by that time the damage to his reputation was done, as the Patriots assumed that he had ordered the massacre.

June 8, 1780

Clinton sailed north, leaving Cornwallis in command of British troops in the South.

June 8, 1780

Lt. Col. Thomas Brown and the King's Carolina Rangers retook Augusta, Georgia, for the British.

June 20, 1780

The Battle of Ramseur's (Ramsour's) Mill, North Carolina. Fought at the site of modern-day Lincolnton, this small but important battle was a clash between Patriot and Loyalist militia. Cornwallis had sent representatives into the backcountry, seeking to have them organize and muster in sync with his planned advance into North Carolina. Some of the Loyalists in western North Carolina ignored the British general's instructions to bide their time for the present, and organized early, unsupported by the British regulars. At Ramseur's Mill, this force of Loyalists under the command of Lt. Col. John Moore was confronted by a Patriot militia under the command of Col. Francis Locke. Both sides were not particularly well-organized, with numbers of men lacking weapons. Nevertheless, an

A North Carolina militiaman. Members of the militia were victorious over their Loyalist counterparts at the Battle of Ramseur's (Ramsour's) Mill in June 1780. Illustration by Stephen Marchesi.

intense fight ensued which ended when the Loyalists retreated. If the Loyalists had organized when requested, they would have probably joined the ranks of Maj. Patrick Ferguson's men and made it a more formidable force during Cornwallis's first invasion of North Carolina.

July 1780–March 1784

The international side of the Revolutionary War continued to expand with the beginning of the Second Anglo-Mysore War in southern India in July 1780. Hyder Ali, ruler of the Indian state of Mysore and an ally of the French, opened the conflict by attacking various British posts. Both the British and French subsequently committed troops and ships to the conflict. The war proved to be a further strain on Britain's military resources.

July 12, 1780

The Battle of Williamston Plantation, South Carolina (Huck's Defeat). A detachment from Tarleton's Legion, under the command of Capt. Christian Huck, sent into the Catawba River Valley to arrest Patriot leaders and secure loyalty to the Crown, was attacked in their camp shortly after sunrise and defeated by a Patriot force under Col. William Bratton in this clash in York County.

July 21, 1780

Skirmish at Colson's Mill, located at the juncture of the Pee Dee and Rocky Rivers, in Montgomery (modern Stanly) County between Patriot and Loyalist militia. The Patriots drove the Loyalists from the field after a short but sharp fight.

July 25, 1780

Horatio Gates took formal command of the forces of the Southern Department at Deep River, North Carolina.

July 30, 1780

Patriot forces consisting of North Carolina, Georgia, and South Carolina militia under Col. Isaac Shelby, Col. Andrew Hamilton, and Col. Elijah Clark captured Thicketty Fort (Fort Anderson), seven miles southeast of Cowpens, South Carolina, and its garrison of ninety-six Loyalists.

August 1, 1780

The Battle of Rocky Mount, South Carolina, and the First Battle of Hanging Rock, South Carolina. A 600–man Loyalist militia force under Lt. Col. George Turnbull repulsed a force of Patriot militia half its size under the command of Col. Thomas Sumter. As part of a diversion, Sumter sent Maj. William Richardson Davie of North Carolina to attack a Loyalist camp at Hanging Rock in Lancaster County, South Carolina, on the same date. Davie captured a number of horses and weapons and routed three companies of Loyalist mounted infantry outside of the fortified post. As Hanging Rock was the northernmost British post in the state, and a key part of its defensive chain stretching from Charleston to Augusta, it was quickly reinforced following news of the clash.

August 6, 1780

The Second Battle of Hanging Rock, South Carolina. Col. Thomas Sumter and a force of 800 Patriot militia attacked an encampment of 1,400 Loyalist troops and militia under Maj. John Carden. The clash is considered a Patriot victory, as they surprised the Loyalists and inflicted more casualties than they received; however, the Loyalists were able to form a square, supported by artillery, and were not driven from the field.

August 9, 1780

Cornwallis launched a campaign to subdue the rest of the Carolinas, marching northward from Charleston to confront the Continental forces under Gates.

August 16, 1780

The Battle of Camden, South Carolina. Cornwallis routed a larger Continental force under the command of Gates. The North Carolina militia, organized in three brigades under the command of Gen. Richard Caswell, formed part of the Patriot line. Two of the three brigades broke and fled shortly after the Virginia militia had similarly fled, leaving the Continental forces to be flanked; the remaining regiment stood its ground. Gates's reputation was damaged as a result of the disaster.

August 18, 1780

Skirmish at Fishing Creek (Catawba Ford), South Carolina. The clash occurred near the convergence of Fishing Creek with the Catawba River, in the Camden District (modern Chester County). Banastre Tarleton

Lt. Gen. Charles, Lord Cornwallis, commander of the British forces in the Carolinas Campaign. A proven veteran officer, who served in many of the campaigns in the Northern states, Cornwallis's weaknesses as a general emerged when he was given independent command of the South. Thomas Gainsborough, 1783, Charles Cornwallis, 1st Marquess Cornwallis, oil on canvas, 29.4. x 24.4 in., National Portrait Gallery, London, accessed Feb. 26, 2026, https://commons.wikimedia.org/wiki/File:Lord_Cornwallis.jpg

and 160 cavalrymen from his British Legion surprised the camp of Col. Thomas Sumter, consisting of 400 South Carolina militiamen, 300 North Carolina militiamen, and 100 Maryland Continentals. Tarleton completely routed Sumter's force, killing over 150 and capturing more than 300. Sumter himself barely escaped.

August 18 or 19, 1780

The Battle of Musgrove Mill, South Carolina. A Patriot force of North Carolina, South Carolina, and Georgia militia under Col. Isaac Shelby, Col. James Williams, and Col. Elijah Clark defeated a larger force of Loyalist regulars and militia under the command of Lt. Col. Alexander Innis near a crossing of the Enoree River. Although victorious, the Patriots withdrew upon receiving word immediately after the battle of the Patriot defeat at Camden. Shelby's men, pursued by Maj. Patrick Ferguson's Loyalists, covered sixty miles in two days in their escape into what is now Tennessee.

August 20, 21, or 25, 1780

Skirmish at Nelson's Ferry (Greater Savannah), in the Charles Town District (modern Orangeburg County), South Carolina, the first of Lt. Col. Francis Marion's victories over British or Loyalist forces. Marion and a small force attacked a small British command escorting captured Patriot prisoners and freed them in a clash near Nelson's Ferry on the Santee River. As in the case of a number of the smaller clashes in the war, the exact date of this event is uncertain.

September 2, 1780

Maj. Patrick Ferguson and his Loyalist command departed from Cornwallis's camp at Camden, South Carolina, to advance into western North Carolina. His mission was to protect the left flank of the main British column, under Cornwallis himself, as it advanced northward, and to rouse the Carolina backcountry to the British standard.

September 4, 1780

Skirmish at Blue Savannah, South Carolina. Francis Marion routed a Loyalist force under Maj. Micajah Ganey in this skirmish near the Pee Dee River.

September 5–12, 1780

The General Assembly convened in New Bern after the Patriot defeat at Camden, South Carolina. It formed a "Board of War" to oversee North Carolina's military efforts.

September 6–October 4, 1780

As a result of Marion's victories, Cornwallis dispatched Maj. James Wemyss, of the 63rd Regiment of Foot to pacify the region between the Santee and Pee Dee Rivers. Wemyss' resulting expedition, which included men from his own regiment, troops from a North Carolina Provincial unit, and Loyalist militiamen, earned him a reputation for brutality second only to Tarleton among Patriot supporters in the Carolinas. Wemyss's men burned at least fifty homes, as well as a Presbyterian church that he claimed supported insurrectionary activity, and hung at least one man. An outnumbered Marion, meanwhile, wisely chose to avoid a clash with Wemyss. Marion dismissed the majority of his men, and left a small group to keep an eye on Wemyss. With around sixty men, he withdrew into North Carolina. Wemyss's campaign cowed some Patriot support in the region but only enraged others, and as soon as he returned to Camden in October, Marion reoccupied the region and began operating again.

September 7, 1780

Cornwallis began his advance from Camden to North Carolina, with Hillsborough as his intended immediate goal. The movement marked the beginning of the unraveling of the British strategy in the South. While advancing into North Carolina, if and when possible, was always part of the British plan to retake the South, Clinton emphasized that it was contingent upon Cornwallis achieving his primary objective: the subjugation of South Carolina. Only when sufficient Loyalists were recruited and organized into militia units, would British troops be replaced at important military posts of the state, should Cornwallis advance into North Carolina. The latter, however, now advanced not only when the number of Loyalists joining the British cause was insufficient, but also while the South Carolina backcountry was still in considerable unrest.

September 7, 1780

Following his instructions from Cornwallis to cover the British general's left flank, Ferguson arrived at Gilbert Town, fifty miles west of Charlotte, in Rutherford County, and established it as his base of operations in western North Carolina.

September 10, 1780

According to an 1823 pamphlet published by Isaac Shelby, Maj. Patrick Ferguson released a Patriot prisoner on or about this date with a message to Shelby and other leaders of the so-called "Overmountain Men," warning that he would launch a campaign into the mountains, hang their leaders, and devastate the countryside if they refused to put down their arms and affirm loyalty to the King. There is no contemporary evidence for the message, and the 1823 Shelby pamphlet was the first indication of its supposed existence. If issued, the message had the opposite effect to what was intended, as it spurred the Overmountain Men to greater resistance in defense of their families and homes. However, it is likely that the message was apocryphal, especially as Ferguson had issued a rather lenient amnesty proposal for those willing to make an oath of allegiance to the King just the preceding day. Instead, it is more probable that the presence of Ferguson's force in the area, constituting a major threat to local Patriot forces, was the reason for the gathering of the Overmountain Men to oppose him.

September 12, 1780

Skirmish at Cane Creek, in Burke County. Patriot forces under Col. Charles McDowell ambushed the Loyalist force of Maj. Patrick Ferguson. McDowell was forced to retreat, leading Ferguson to conclude inaccurately that Patriot resistance in the backcountry was finished.

September 14–18, 1780

First Siege of Augusta, Georgia. A Patriot militia force under Lt. Col. Elijah Clark besieged Augusta, defended by British-born Georgia Loyalist Lt. Col. Thomas Brown, commander of the King's Carolina Rangers (formerly the East Florida Rangers). The Loyalists were supported by Creek and Cherokee allies. Brown sent word of his plight to Lt. Col. John Harris Cruger of the 1st Battalion, DeLancey's Brigade, a New York Loyalist unit, who was in command at Ninety-Six. Cruger took most his garrison and marched with 500 men to Brown's relief. On their approach, Clark withdrew and retreated about fifty miles northwest of Augusta to Wilkes County, Georgia, but eventually fell back into South Carolina when Cruger followed and burned the homes of Patriot supporters in the area and hung those believed to have broken paroles, per instructions left behind by Cornwallis. Likewise, Brown hung Patriot prisoners captured at Augusta believed to be parolees, while others were killed by the Indians.

September 21, 1780

Patriot Col. William Richardson Davie of Salisbury attacked and routed a party of Loyalists from Tarleton's Legion at Wauchope's (frequently spelled Wahab's) Plantation in northwestern York County, South Carolina (some place the location in modern southwestern Union County), on this date.

September 25, 1780

Cornwallis, hoping to mop up the remaining Patriot forces that escaped from Camden, and expecting the backcountry to flock to the British standard, crossed the border into North Carolina.

September 25, 1780

Overmountain militia from Virginia under the command of Col. William Campbell, from North Carolina under the command of

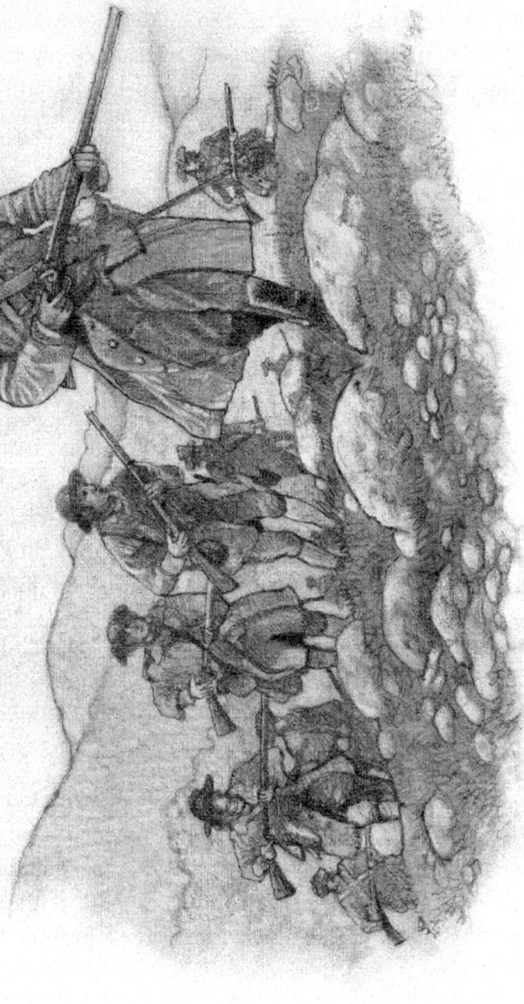

Overmountain Men from beyond the Appalachians. Many gathered in the fall of 1780 to resist the expedition of Maj. Patrick Ferguson into western North Carolina, where he hoped to suppress Patriot resistance and rally Loyalists to the British standard. Illustration by Stephen Marchesi.

Maj. Joseph McDowell, and from what is now eastern Tennessee under the command of Col. Isaac Shelby and Colonel John Sevier, rendezvoused at Sycamore Shoals on the Watauga River in what is now Tennessee on this date in order to fight the Loyalist force of Maj. Patrick Ferguson.

September 26, 1780

Skirmish at Charlotte, North Carolina. Patriot forces under Col. William Richardson Davie sought to hinder Cornwallis's advance northward. Davie's men repulsed charges by Tarleton's cavalry twice with well-aimed volleys, but the charge of the British infantry was more successful than the cavalry and the Patriots withdrew.

September 28 or 29, 1780

Skirmish at Black Mingo, Georgetown District (modern Georgetown County), South Carolina. Col. John Coming Ball and a small force of Loyalists were attacked and routed by Lt. Col. Francis Marion in a brief clash.

September 30, 1780

The Overmountain Men from the Sycamore Shores rendezvous camped at Quaker Meadows, the plantation home of Col. Charles McDowell, near Morganton, and met with more North Carolina militiamen under Col. Benjamin Cleveland and Maj. Joseph Winston. On this same date, Ferguson received word from Patriot deserters that militia forces from the backcountry were gathering against his command. On the following day, Ferguson began to retreat in order to unite with Cornwallis at Charlotte.

October 3, 1780

"The Battle of the Bees," a skirmish in Mecklenburg County. A Loyalist foraging party was pillaging local farms when some of their men accidentally knocked over a beehive, whose enraged inhabitants fell to stinging the Loyalists. While this was going on, Patriot militia under Capt. James Thompson attacked the foragers. The Loyalists drove the Patriots off but were sniped at from men in concealment along the roadside throughout their march back to Charlotte.

A nurse tends a wounded Patriot soldier. Medical conditions in the Revolutionary War were poor, and doctors relied on assistance from local women who often tended to wounded soldiers, especially injured members of their own family or community. Illustration by Stephen Marchesi.

October 5–6, 1780

The Overmountain Men, by now numbering about 1,400 men, camped at Alexander's Ford on Green River in Rutherford County, North Carolina on this date. The militiamen were heading in the wrong direction, believing that Ferguson was retreating toward Ninety-Six, and were unaware that he had turned eastward in an effort to unite with Cornwallis at Charlotte. In the early morning hours of October 6, Col. Edward Lacey of South Carolina arrived at the Alexander's Ford campsite with news that Ferguson's actual whereabouts were in the vicinity of Kings Mountain. The Overmountain Men made the decision to rendezvous at Cowpens with a South Carolina force under Col. James Williams, before moving on to Kings Mountain.

October 7, 1780

The Battle of Kings Mountain, South Carolina. The Overmountain Men entrapped Ferguson's command at Kings Mountain and launched a surprise attack. Although the Loyalists repulsed the assaults of various Patriot commands, the latter regrouped and attacked again and again, gradually moved up the ridge and gained the top, and pushed the Loyalists back into their campsite. Attempts by the Loyalists to break out failed, and Ferguson was killed in the fighting, leading to their surrender. Partly due to confusion on the Patriot side about the surrender, and partly due to the desire of some to avenge the killings of Patriots after previous battles, some Loyalists were killed as they attempted to surrender. The battle represented the first major reversal of British military success in the South in some time, and proved to be a major turning point in the campaign.

October 9, 1780

Skirmish at Polk's Mill, in Mecklenburg County. Cornwallis established a post at the Polk grist mill, west of Charlotte, to use as a foraging base. On this date, Col. Philip Taylor led a band of 120 men from the North Carolina Mounted Volunteers Regiment of Cavalry, along with a detachment from the Granville County Militia Regiment, both from the Hillsborough District Brigade of North Carolina Militia, to capture the mill at night. The garrison consisted of twenty men from the Royal Welsh Fusiliers and some local Loyalist militiamen, all under the command of 2nd Lt. Stephen Guyon of the Fusiliers. The British and Loyalist force inside the fortified mill drove the Patriots off.

October 14–29, 1780

Cornwallis evacuated Charlotte on October 14 and marched toward Winnsborough, South Carolina. The decision to withdraw was largely the result of Kings Mountain. Not only had the British failed to successfully raise a large Loyalist force to support their operations, but with the destruction of Ferguson's command, the British were open to a possible flanking movement by the Patriots. In addition, the area around Charlotte was too unstable to use as an advanced post, and Cornwallis's communication links with South Carolina and Georgia were endangered. The British withdrawal was hastened by fears that they were threatened by a 5,000-man militia force under the command of Brig. Gen. William Lee Davidson. Thirty supply wagons were abandoned outside of Charlotte to speed up the march. The alarm was based on bad intelligence, as Davidson

The death of Maj. Patrick Ferguson at the Battle of Kings Mountain, South Carolina. The battle was a major turning point in the Carolinas Campaign and was the first major Patriot victory in the campaign after a series of defeats. The destruction of Ferguson's force by the Overmountain Men forced Cornwallis to abandon Charlotte and retreat into South Carolina. Alonzo Chappel, 1863, Death of Maj. Ferguson at Kings Mountain, engraving, Anne S. K. Brown Collection, Brown University, Providence, R.I., accessed Feb. 26, 2026, https://commons.wikimedia.org/wiki/File:KingsMountain_DeathOfFerguson_Chappel.jpg

had no more than 300 men with him. The decision to abandon the wagons proved costly, as the British soon suffered from the lack of supplies, forcing them to forage on the march. In addition, some British officers behaved harshly toward Loyalist militia officers, causing many Loyalists accompanying the British to desert. Besides Davidson, the British were pursued for several days by the militia company of Mounted Volunteers under Capt. William Richardson Davie. Cornwallis's command arrived at Winnsborough on October 29, minus a detachment sent to Camden.

October 14, 1780

Skirmish at Shallow Ford in Surry (modern-day Yadkin) County, near modern Huntsville, fought on the same day as the British evacuation of Charlotte. The engagement arose as a band of Loyalist militia, raised in Surry County under the command of Col. Gideon Wright, moved along the Great Wagon Road in the direction of Charlotte, hoping to join Cornwallis's force. The Loyalists, who had been raiding the homes of Patriot supporters east of the Appalachians, had attracted attention in both North Carolina and Virginia. From Virginia, a Patriot force of state militia under Maj. Joseph Cloyd marched south, originally intending to join the Overmountain Men and fight Ferguson, but after hearing of the latter's defeat and death, they altered their target to Wright's Loyalists. In North Carolina, meanwhile, additional Patriot forces gathered under the command of Col. Joseph Williams. The Loyalist route of march led them to Shallow Ford on the Yadkin River. There, they were intercepted by Cloyd's Virginians, who were soon reinforced by Williams. After a sharp fight, the Loyalists were driven off. The repulse of the Loyalist militia, along with the earlier loss of Ferguson's command, deprived Cornwallis of additional troops as the Carolinas Campaign progressed.

October 14, 1780

Nathanael Greene, quartermaster general of the Continental Army, was appointed to succeed Gates as commander of Continental forces in the Southern Department.

October, 1780

Incident at Gilbert Town. During the British withdrawal from Charlotte to Winnsborough, a small party of South Carolina militiamen on the Patriot side entered North Carolina in search of Loyalist officer Capt. James Dunlap, commander of Ferguson's advanced guard at

Cane Creek who was wounded in that action. The militiamen, commanded by Capt. James Gillespie, sought revenge on Dunlap for executing some of their comrades and, it was said, for kidnapping Gillespie's fiancé, who died in captivity. On an unknown date believed to have been in October, the militiamen gained access to the house where Dunlap was recovering under a false pretext. On finding that his fiancée was dead, Gillespie shot Dunlap in bed—or so the story went. Regardless, and for whatever reason, Gillespie shot Dunlap and left him for dead. Dunlap survived, however, and was taken by friends to Ninety-Six, where he recovered and bedeviled the Patriots forces later on.

October 22–November 18, 1780

Maj. Gen. Alexander Leslie was sent from New York with a 2,500-man expeditionary force to Virginia to act as a diversion from Cornwallis's entry into entered North Carolina. Clinton ordered the expedition at a time when he had not yet received word of Ferguson's defeat at Kings Mountain. Once he arrived in Virginia, Leslie fell subject to Cornwallis's direct command. Leslie landed at Portsmouth on October 22 and launched a series of raids on the coast and along the James River. The small Continental and militia forces under Brig. Gen. Peter Muhlenberg could do little to stop him. In November, Leslie received orders from Cornwallis to join him in North Carolina by sailing to the Cape Fear River and marching for a junction at Cross Creek. He departed Virginia on November 18. When he arrived off the Cape Fear, however, Leslie found ships waiting with fresh instructions from Cornwallis to sail to Charleston and march overland through the backcountry to reinforce him. Leslie arrived at Charleston on December 14, and encamped at Camden, some forty miles from Winnsborough, on January 1.

October 25 or 26, 1780

The Battle of Tearcoat Swamp, Camden District, South Carolina. Francis Marion and a force of about 150 men struck a force of nearly 200 newly-recruited Loyalists under Col. Samuel Tynes in the early morning hours in their camp and routed them.

November 3, 1780

Skirmish at Northwest River Bridge, Virginia. Lt. Col. John (Johann) Christian Senf, Horatio Gates's engineer and Scandinavian-born resident of South Carolina, who was on a surveying assignment in southeastern

Virginia at the time of Leslie's invasion, commanded Patriot forces in this action. Modern-day retellings place the action in the portion of Bladen County, North Carolina, that is now Robeson County, and state that Senf led a force of ninety or ninety-one members of the Camden Regiment of South Carolina militia in a successful attack on a Loyalist post. Various contemporary documents, including Senf's own account given in a letter dated November 5 and published in *The State Records of North Carolina*, place the location of the clash near the Northwest River Bridge in southeastern Virginia. Senf previously commanded Virginia militia in an action at the Great Bridge on the Elizabeth River on October 28 and had been driven back to the Northwest River Bridge, where he requested reinforcements from the North Carolina militia. On November 3, the British attacked and drove off the Virginia militia guarding the Northwest River Bridge, forcing Senf to withdraw forces from another post eight miles away and unite his command to prevent it from being cut off. When the clash was over, he was able to gather only 140 Virginia and North Carolina militiamen. By November 5, when he took a new position in the Great Dismal Swamp, desertion had sapped this force down to less than thirty men. Following the action, Senf attempted to get further reinforcements from the North Carolina militia, with what success is unknown; although other documents indicate that Leslie's arrival in Virginia caused a panic in northeastern North Carolina, and that there were difficulties gathering militia forces as far south as Edenton.

November 5–14, 1780

Cornwallis, frustrated by the growing unrest in the South Carolina backcountry, dispatched Banastre Tarleton to deal with Francis Marion. Tarleton initially attempted to lure Marion into a trap, but the latter was forewarned by Mary Richardson, the recently widowed wife of Patriot Brig. Gen. Richard Richardson, and he took his command northeast from the Santee River to Benbow's Ferry on the Black River. There he decided to give battle to Tarleton; the latter, however, having pursued Marion for nearly thirty miles, elected not to plunge too deeply into the swamp country. Instead, Tarleton launched a harsh campaign of repression, burning homes and crops of known or suspected Patriot supporters.

November 9, 1780

Skirmish at Fishdam Ford, Camden District (Chester County), South Carolina. Major James Wemyss of the 63rd Regiment of Foot received word that Thomas Sumter, now a brigadier general in the South Carolina militia, was camped at Moore's Mill on the Broad River with a command of between 400 and 600 men. Weymss received permission from Cornwallis to lead a force of a hundred mounted infantry and forty dragoons from Tarleton's Legion to attack Sumter's camp at dawn on November 9. Leaving Winnsborough on the night of November 8, Wemyss reached Moore's Mill at midnight to find that Sumter had moved camp five miles downstream to Fishdam Ford. Disregarding Cornwallis's orders to not launch a night attack, Wemyss reached Sumter's camp at 1 a.m. and pushed forward. He promptly ran into the Patriot pickets, who shot him off his horse. Wemyss's second-in-command, Lt. Henry Stark, led a charge into the camp, and finding the Patriots had withdrawn, the British and Loyalists began to loot it. Sumter himself played no role in the fight, as he fled and hid while Tarleton's dragoons converged on his tent. His subordinate commanders took charge. Unexpectedly, the Patriots fired out of the darkness, with the British fully visible in the campfires. Stark withdrew, then ordered the now dismounted infantry to launch a bayonet charge, but they were repulsed by Patriot fire. Stark was forced to withdraw, leaving his dead and wounded behind, including Wemyss, who was captured. Although the Patriot victory was credited to Sumter, the skirmish was won by his subordinates and their men.

November 20, 1780

Skirmish at Blackstock's Farm, Ninety-Six District (modern Union County), South Carolina. In the wake of Weymss's defeat at Fishdam Ford, Cornwallis ordered Tarleton to abandon hunting Marion and concentrate on destroying Sumter. Although a poor strategist and tactician with an outsized opinion of himself, and an inability to cooperate with other guerilla leaders or obey departmental commanders such as Gates and Greene, Sumter was a natural-born leader in the sense that he was able to inspire men to follow him no matter what; and his raids had proven to be a major annoyance to the British. He now commanded around a thousand men. Tarleton meanwhile set out with a force of 300 British regulars and 200 provincial Loyalist regulars. Encountering Sumter's men on November 18, Tarleton drove Sumter backward the following day. Sumter withdrew to Blackstock's Farm, located in the hills above the Tyger River, and set up a strong defensive position, which would force Tarleton to attack uphill against the Patriots lined up behind rail fences and in the farmhouse itself with a clear field of fire. When Tarleton arrived late in the afternoon, he recklessly attacked before his full force had arrived and suffered heavy casualties. Sumter was wounded by a volley from the 63rd Regiment of Foot and carried off the field; he would be out of action for two months. Tarleton withdrew to regroup for a fresh attack the next day but found that the Patriots had withdrawn overnight. It was Tarleton's first defeat, and he lied in his report to Cornwallis that he had in fact won, although admitting that he had suffered heavy casualties.

December 3, 1780

Greene took formal command of the Southern Department in Charlotte.

December 1780–Summer 1781

As Greene and Cornwallis maneuvered through the Carolinas, their armies and their camp followers brought smallpox with them. Fresh outbreaks of the disease occurred in Salem and other neighboring villages beginning in December 1780, followed by one among British prisoners at Salisbury in January 1781. By spring, there were reports of major outbreaks in Campbelltown (modern Fayetteville), Hillsborough, and Halifax. Among the Patriot forces the disease struck worse among the militiamen, who were not inoculated. Greene worried that the expense of inoculating so many militiamen, as well as the fact that it would slow down his movements to do so, was counterproductive and instead decided to send many of the militia home. Meanwhile, the British troops struggled with outbreaks of malaria and yellow fever, diseases which much of the local population had already developed immunity to through repeated exposure over decades.

December 16, 1780

Faced with an army that was too large to subsist in the Charlotte area, Greene decided to divide it into two segments. Although it was normally considered to be a bad military practice to divide one's forces in the face of an enemy army, it made good sense from a supply perspective. In the long run it paid off for Greene. While Greene kept the main body of his command with him at Charlotte, he detached a small segment under the command of veteran officer Daniel Morgan with orders to cross the

Maj. Gen. Nathanael Greene, a veteran officer who served under George Washington for most of the war, was selected by the Continental Congress to replace Horatio Gates as commander of the Southern Department of the Continental Army following Gates's defeat at the Battle of Camden. He faced a critical situation, as the Continental Army in the South was demoralized and disorganized after Camden, and the British controlled much of Georgia and South Carolina. Greene set about rebuilding the army. He subsequently wore down the British army in a war of attrition by withdrawing in the face of British advances, stretching the British supply lines, and striking when conditions were advantageous. Charles Wilson Peale, 1783, Nathanael Greene, oil on canvas, 23 x 19 in., National Park Service, accessed 26 Feb. 2026, https://commons.wikimedia.org/wiki/File:Greene_portrait.jpg

Catawba River, harass whatever British or Loyalist forces were in the area, and gather supplies. Morgan's force included Maryland and Delaware Continental units, a force of Virginia riflemen, and a detachment of dragoons under William Washington.

December 20, 1780

The outbreak of the Fourth Anglo-Dutch War. On September 3, a British warship had captured a ship off the coast of Newfoundland carrying Henry Laurens, U.S. minister to the Netherlands. The British retrieved Laurens's papers, which he had thrown into the ocean, that included an unauthorized 1778 draft treaty negotiated by U.S. diplomat

William Lee and powerful Amsterdam banker Jean de Neufville for an alliance between the two nations. The papers also revealed that Laurens was on a mission to borrow 10 million guilders from the Netherlands. Matters were already tense between the old allies as British warships had been waylaying and boarding Dutch trading vessels for some time, fueled by the knowledge of secret Dutch trade with both the United States and France. The Dutch then rushed to join Catherine the Great's League of Armed Neutrality in December. In response, the British declared war on the Dutch Republic, citing a number of incidents not related to the neutrality issue to argue that the Dutch were not really neutral, thus preventing conflict with the nations of the League. As in the case of Spain, the Dutch would not formally ally with the United States, but Britain once again had to further stretch its military and economic resources as a result of the expansion of the Revolutionary War.

December 21, 1780

Morgan and his detachment marched from Charlotte. By Christmas Day, he reached the Pacolet River in South Carolina, crossed at Grindall's Ford, and established a camp. He was now on the left flank of Cornwallis's main force, headquartered at Winnsborough, where Cornwallis made preparations for a return invasion of North Carolina. Morgan was soon reinforced by Patriot militia under the command of Andrew Pickens.

December 30–31, 1780

Skirmish at Hammond's Store and capture of Williams' Fort, South Carolina. Upon his arrival west of the Pacolet River, Morgan became aware of a Loyalist militia force, said to be from Georgia, that was preying upon Patriot residents in the region. He sent William Washington and his dragoons, accompanied by militia, to deal with the marauders. Washington pursued the Loyalists to Hammond's Store, where on December 30 he attacked and routed them. Many of Washington's men showed no quarter to their opponents. Washington then moved to rejoin Morgan, although a detachment from his command advanced on the Loyalist post of Williams' Fort to the south of Hammond's Store on December 31. Accounts vary as to what precisely happened and whether the Loyalists had already abandoned the post before the detachment's arrival, but most agree that the Patriots burned it. These otherwise minor incidents had repercussions, however, as the retreating Loyalists fell back to Ninety-Six and notified Cornwallis, convincing him that the latter position was (incorrectly) under threat by Morgan's command. Cornwallis ordered Tarleton on January 1 to take his legion to Ninety-Six, confront Morgan, and force him back across the Broad River.

January 1–19, 1781

Following Leslie's departure from Virginia to join Cornwallis, Sir Henry Clinton decided to send another expedition to the Chesapeake. He ordered Brig. Gen. Benedict Arnold, former Patriot hero and now a traitor to his old cause, in command of 1,800 men to capture Portsmouth, gain the support of local Loyalists, and interrupt the supply chain from the North supporting Greene's army. Arnold's force, consisting of a mixture of Scottish, Hessian, and Loyalist units, sailed from New York City on December 20, 1780. On January 1, they began to ascend the James River. They seized Richmond, the state capital, on January 5 after a brief skirmish with Virginia militia. Arnold offered terms to Gov. Thomas Jefferson to spare the city if all the merchants' vessels in the James River between Richmond and Westover, loaded with tobacco, wine, and other goods enumerated by Arnold, were turned over to him; he would even pay the merchants half the value of their goods. Jefferson refused, however, and Arnold ordered his men to sack Richmond. They burned much of it on January 6. Arnold's force then marched downriver to Westover, plundering the countryside as they went. On January 10, he reembarked his men and moved to Portsmouth, arriving on January 19, and set it up as his base per Clinton's instructions.

January 1–16, 1781

Following Cornwallis's orders, Tarleton and his men moved toward Ninety-Six. Tarleton's intelligence gathering soon led to the realization that Ninety-Six was not threatened, and also uncovered the general whereabouts of Morgan's command. Halting his force well short of its destination, Tarleton sent a message to Cornwallis advising him of the situation and proposing a plan of action. Tarleton requested reinforcements. After their arrival, he then would cross the Broad River and advance on Morgan. Cornwallis would meanwhile march up the east bank of the Broad. If all went as planned, Morgan would be caught between two forces and defeated, depriving Greene of an important part of his army. Cornwallis sent an additional regiment to Tarleton, who then crossed the Broad at Brierly's Ferry on January 2. Cornwallis began his own advance up the Broad on January 7. The latter movement convinced Greene that the British were about to reenter North Carolina. Morgan, meanwhile, retreated northward toward the Broad on January 14, pulling Tarleton away from Cornwallis in the process. Tarleton drove his men hard in pursuit, bringing them closer and closer to Morgan but wearing them out as he did so. On January 16, Morgan arrived at Hannah's Cowpens, just south of the Broad, and decided to make a stand against Tarleton.

January 5–7, 1781

Battle at the Village, West Florida (modern Daphne, Alabama), a failed attempt by the British in Pensacola to recapture Mobile, fought at a village on the eastern shore of Mobile Bay. The British were repulsed after several assaults on the Spanish intrenchments.

January 6, 1781

Battle of Jersey, a failed attempt by the French to capture the English Channel island of Jersey, a base for British privateering operations against French, Spanish, and American shipping. The French landed 1,400 troops, but they were repulsed by the British troops defending the island.

January 16, 1781

Cornwallis camped at Turkey Creek in northern South Carolina.

January 17, 1781

The Battle of Cowpens, South Carolina. Tarleton woke his command at 2:00 in the morning and put them in pursuit of Morgan. After a difficult march through rough terrain in the dark, they arrived at Cowpens before sunrise, and found Morgan already deployed to meet them. The Patriot position seemed ripe for another rout by Tarleton, as the terrain consisted of open fields interspersed with patches of woodland, and no points upon which Morgan could anchor his flanks, leaving them open to attack by cavalry. If defeated, the Patriots could be driven into the Broad River, if Tarleton's cavalry did not sweep around and cut them off from retreat first. Morgan deployed his command in a defense in depth, a formation arrayed in a series of receding lines intended to wear out an attacking force. A skirmish line of 120 North Carolina and Georgia militiamen spread out across a broad front made up the first line. Armed with rifles and intended to act as sharpshooters, they were instructed to open fire when Tarleton's men got within fifty yards, targeting officers in particular, and then withdraw to the second line, commanded by Pickens.

The Battle of Cowpens, S.C., was the second major turning point in the Southern campaign. Greene divided his army in order to feed it better, sending one section under Daniel Morgan into South Carolina. Banastre Tarleton proposed to Cornwallis that the British should trap and destroy this isolated wing. Tarleton, expecting an easy victory, attempted to destroy Morgan's force on his own, but his attack broke on Morgan's tactical plan of positioning his army in three lines which successively bled the British before withdrawing to join the next line. Tarleton was routed and barely avoided capture, while most of his force was captured or killed. Wikimedia Commons /Public Domain.

This position, made up of 300 South Carolina militiamen, to be reinforced by the retreating first line, would fire two volleys before withdrawing to the left and reforming behind the third line. This force was made up of 600 men, and consisted of Morgan's best troops, units from the Maryland and Delaware Continental Line, backed up by Virginia and Georgia militiamen with veteran experience. William Washington's cavalry was placed to the rear. When Tarleton arrived, he quickly deployed his force and advanced without reconnoitering the Patriot position. A British cavalry charge was repulsed by the skirmishers, who fired on the following infantry attack before withdrawing to the second line. The second line fired its two volleys, inflicting heavy casualties, and then withdrew to the left. Tarleton assumed that a rout had begun and attacked the third line. The veteran Continentals and militiamen checked the advance and counterattacked. As the British and Loyalists gave way, Washington's cavalry attacked their right, while Pickens and the reformed militiamen of the first two lines hit their left. Tarleton's force collapsed, and he barely escaped capture or death when he was attacked by Washington in person. The battle, which lasted only about an hour, was a major turning point in the Southern campaign.

January 18–February 15, 1781

The "Race to the Dan." In the wake of Cowpens, Cornwallis determined to catch Morgan, and reinforced with fresh troops from Charleston, set out in pursuit. Morgan barely got away, and was joined by Greene, who had ridden ahead of his army, on January 30. The main body of Greene's army was already moving north toward Salisbury, where his forces could resupply. A series of hard marches lay ahead, in which Greene always managed to keep at least barely ahead of Cornwallis. In the process, Cornwallis's supply lines to South Carolina were increasingly stretched, putting a hardship on the British and Loyalist troops. The march was marked by several skirmishes, mostly the contesting of river crossings by Greene's rear guard. Greene reached Salisbury on February 2, then continued northward to reunite with the rest of his army a few days later. The Continental forces finally crossed the Dan River on February 13–14, making sure all boats in the area ended up on their side. The British arrived on February 15, unable to cross. Greene now had a chance to rest and regroup his forces, before moving southward again.

Brigadier General Daniel Morgan, victor at the Battle of Cowpens. Morgan was a native of New Jersey who settled in Virginia and was a veteran of frontier warfare. Earlier in the war, he served in the invasion of Canada and the Saratoga Campaign. He joined the Continental Army in the South following the Battle of Camden. After Greene assumed command, he was given the task of taking half of Greene's army into South Carolina to feed it. Pursued by Tarleton and Cornwallis, who attempted to trap him between two British forces, Morgan faced Tarleton's command at Cowpens and defeated it before moving to rejoin the rest of Greene's army in the "Race to the Dan." Charles Wilson Peale, ca. 1794, Daniel Morgan, oil on canvas, Independence National Historical Park, Philadelphia, PA., accessed Feb. 26, 2026, https://commons.wikimedia.org/wiki/File:DanielMorgan.jpeg

January 18, 1781

Cornwallis, encamped at Turkey Creek, was joined by Tarleton in the morning and informed about Cowpens. Later in the day, Leslie and his reinforcements, which had been struggling through the rain-soaked South Carolina Low Country in their march up from Camden, finally reached Cornwallis. Cornwallis did not set out in pursuit of Morgan until the following day.

January 22, 1781

Cornwallis reentered North Carolina in pursuit of Morgan.

January 25, 1781

Cornwallis's army reached Ramsour's Mill on this date and camped for three days. While there, the British general decided to burn his army's baggage train and dispose of anything that would impede a rapid pursuit. The British army, moving further and further from its supply base in South Carolina, endured much hardship as a result of this decision.

January 27–February 14, 1781

The General Assembly met in Halifax. It raised troops and supplies and levied taxes. It also abolished the Board of War and formed the Council Extraordinary to work with Governor Nash.

January 28, 1781

A British expedition under Major James Craig departed Charlestown, South Carolina, on January 21. Acting on orders given by Cornwallis before his departure from South Carolina, the force sailed along the coast and then up the Cape Fear River, capturing Wilmington on January 28. The seizure of the port opened a potential supply and communications route for Cornwallis's command if the British general should move that far east.

January 30, 1781

Skirmish at Heron Bridge, New Hanover County, some ten miles to the northeast of Wilmington. North Carolina. Militia forces withdrawing from Wilmington were reinforced here and decided to make a stand at the bridge. Major Craig led a contingent of men from the 82nd Regiment of Foot and the Royal Marines late in the afternoon for a surprise night attack on the Patriot position. The British routed the militia and then burned the bridge. Following his return to Wilmington, Craig mounted a joint naval and army expedition up the Cape Fear, which captured most of the vessels that fled upriver at the fall of city, seized supplies, and burned local Patriot farms and plantations.

February 1, 1781

Skirmishes at Cowan's Ford and Tarrant's Tavern. Part of the "Race to the Dan." Following Cowpens, Cornwallis pursued Morgan's force as he withdrew to unite with Greene's main command. While Morgan hurried toward the Yadkin River, North Carolina militia forces deployed to defend the fords along the rain-swollen Catawba River in an effort to delay Cornwallis. On the morning of February 1, Cornwallis's men forded the river at Cowan's Ford in northwestern Mecklenburg County, defended by militia forces under the command of Brig. Gen. William Lee Davidson. He was killed and the militia driven off. Tarleton was sent in pursuit, and that afternoon (according to his memoirs; state commemorations often place the incident on the following day) hit and dispersed militia forces regrouping at Tarrant's (Torrance's) Tavern in western Rowan (modern-day Iredell) County. Unbeknownst to Tarleton, Greene was only about six miles away at the farm of David Carr.

February 2, 1781

Greene and a small escort left Carr's farm after midnight and rode on toward Salisbury. Once there, he oversaw the removal of military supplies while Morgan's men marched on in the direction of the Yadkin River (The "Race to the Dan").

February 3, 1781

Crossing of the Yadkin River at Trading Ford, part of the "Race to the Dan," Greene, accompanying Morgan's column, crossed the Yadkin River at Trading Ford in Rowan County. The Patriots took all of the boats with them and secured them on the opposite bank to prevent the British from crossing. The British advanced guard arrived at around midnight and skirmished briefly with the small band of militiamen who were still on that side of the river.

February 3, 1781

St. Eustatius, a major Dutch trading center in the Caribbean, and the center of clandestine Dutch trade with the United States, surrendered to a British fleet under Rear Adm. George Romney. The surprised Dutch were unaware that Britian had declared war in December.

February 4, 1781

Cornwallis and the main body of his army arrived at the Yadkin in the morning to find the Patriot force on the opposite bank and with no boats to aid in crossing. The British artillery shelled the Patriot camp across the river, while Cornwallis sent Tarleton northward to find another crossing. Tarleton was held up for nearly three hours by a force of militia at the bridge over Grant's Creek, but he eventually flanked and dispersed them. Continuing north, he found a crossing point over the Yadkin for the army at Shallow Ford, but it was twenty-five miles away from the Trading Ford (The "Race to the Dan").

February 6–8, 1781

Reunification of the Army of the Southern Department at Guilford Courthouse (modern Greensboro). Part of the "Race to the Dan." Morgan's column reached Guilford Courthouse on February 6, where he was joined by Greene on the next day, who had stayed behind with a small body to keep an eye on Cornwallis. Maj. Gen. Isaac Huger, advancing up from South Carolina with the main body of Greene's army, joined them on February 8. Cornwallis, meanwhile, marched northward toward Shallow Ford on February 6, crossing there on February 7 and resting his army for a day before heading toward Salem. While Greene camped at Guilford Courthouse, Cornwallis reprovisioned his army via foraging among the Moravian communities surrounding Salem.

February 9, 1781

Greene held a council of war with several of his officers to determine whether he should fight Cornwallis at Guilford Courthouse. The officers who participated all argued against fighting a battle, due to the relatively small size of his force as opposed to that of Cornwallis, and also due to the destitute condition of his troops, who were badly equipped, uniformed, and supplied. It was decided that the army would resume its march to Virginia, where it would be resupplied and refitted, and where hopefully militia forces could be recruited for a confrontation with Cornwallis. The latter, meanwhile, closed the gap between his army and Greene's, camping for the night east of Salem.

February 10, 1781

As part of his strategy for retreating to Virginia, Greene decided to organize a diversionary force made up of many of his best troops. These included infantry detachments from the Maryland, Delaware, and Virginia Continental Line units, detachments from the cavalry units of William Washington and Henry Lee, a detachment of infantry from Lee's Legion, and a small force of Virginia riflemen. Command of this unit was offered to Daniel Morgan, but he suffered greatly from hemorrhoids and sciatica and was granted leave by Greene to return to his home in Virginia to recover. Command was then granted to Col. Otho Williams of Greene's staff and the Maryland Continental Line.

The diversionary force would move toward the fords of the upper Dan River in an effort to fool Cornwallis that Greene's entire army was marching in that direction. In the meantime, Greene would lead the main body in the opposite direction, with the intent to cross the Dan at Boyd's and Irvin's Ferry, where Greene's quartermaster general, Col. Edward Carrington, would collect boats for the crossing. The Patriot forces departed on their respective routes on this date. Cornwallis also advanced in the direction of Guilford Courthouse. The next few days would show that he had taken Greene's bait, as he moved in pursuit of Williams's command toward the upper Dan.

February 11, 1781

Skirmish at Bruce's Crossroads (Summerfield), Guilford County. Part of the "Race to the Dan." Dated to February 12 in some sources. Encounter between Tarleton's Legion and the cavalry detachment from Lt. Col. Henry "Light Horse Harry" Lee's Legion, acting as Williams' rearguard, which degenerated into a brutal match when some of Tarleton's men slashed Lee's fourteen-year-old bugler to death. (*Note:* this event is sometimes interpreted by modern-day writers as being one of two separate events taking place on different dates and at different locations, a confusion caused by the scarcity of wartime documentation for this phase of the march and the fact that different participants, writing as much as decades later, often used different names for locations and were not consistent with each other in regards to dating. In this instance, some writers noted an encounter between Tarleton and Lee, the latter acting as Williams's rearguard, on February 8 at Reedy Creek, which has been interpreted by some contemporary writers as a reference to Reedy Creek on the modern-day Davidson-Forsyth County border. However, they are almost certainly confusing Reedy Creek with Reedy Fork Creek, a branch of the Haw River, which lay just south of Summerfield. Further, Williams's force was not activated until February 10, so while Lee could have certainly encountered Tarleton on February 8, it would not have been as part of Williams's command. The two incidents therefore are almost certainly the same encounter, misdated in some accounts to February 8.)

Ca. February 13, 1781

Although the exact date and the reasons are obscure, due to a lack of surviving correspondence and other documents, it is about this time that Cornwallis realized that Greene was heading toward the lower fords of the Dan, rather than the upper fords. The race to the river now began in earnest. Williams's diversionary force became Greene's rearguard.

February 13–14, 1781

Greene crossed the Dan River. The British, who arrived on the morning of February 15, were unable to follow, as the river was swollen by rain and all of the boats had been taken across by the Patriots. Cornwallis was forced with the choice of marching for the upper fords or falling back into North Carolina to regroup.

February 17–20, 1781

Cornwallis withdrew from the Dan River to Hillsborough, North Carolina. Upon arrival, he issued a proclamation calling for Loyalists to volunteer for service. Although there was some initial success, the support soon evaporated as word came of Greene's recrossing the Dan on February 22 and of Pyle's Defeat on February 25.

February 18, 1781 (misdated to February 17 in some modern accounts)

Skirmish at Hart's Mill, Orange County. Capt. Joseph Graham and his mounted company from the Rowan County Militia were dispatched by Andrew Pickens to scout below the Dan. Early on the morning of February 18, they surprised and captured a small British garrison occupying Hart's Mill, located on the Eno River approximately a mile and a half from Hillsborough. The Patriots occupied the mill and were joined there a day later by Lee's Legion, part of a force sent by Greene across the Dan to gather information on Cornwallis's activities.

February 22, 1781

Greene recrossed the Dan and marched south to confront Cornwallis. He was motivated to act by rumors, incorrect as it turned out, that the British were rallying larger numbers of Loyalists to join Cornwallis's command than was in fact the case. Greene, meanwhile, had rested, refitted, and resupplied his army, and its numbers swelled by the arrival of more militia forces from Virginia and North Carolina. The time therefore seemed ripe for a confrontation with Cornwallis before the British general's numbers increased. Given that the rumors of a large Loyalist turnout were false, however, Greene marched south with a decided advantage in numbers. Pressures of a different nature motivated Cornwallis to also seek a decisive showdown. The British, far from their supply base in Camden,

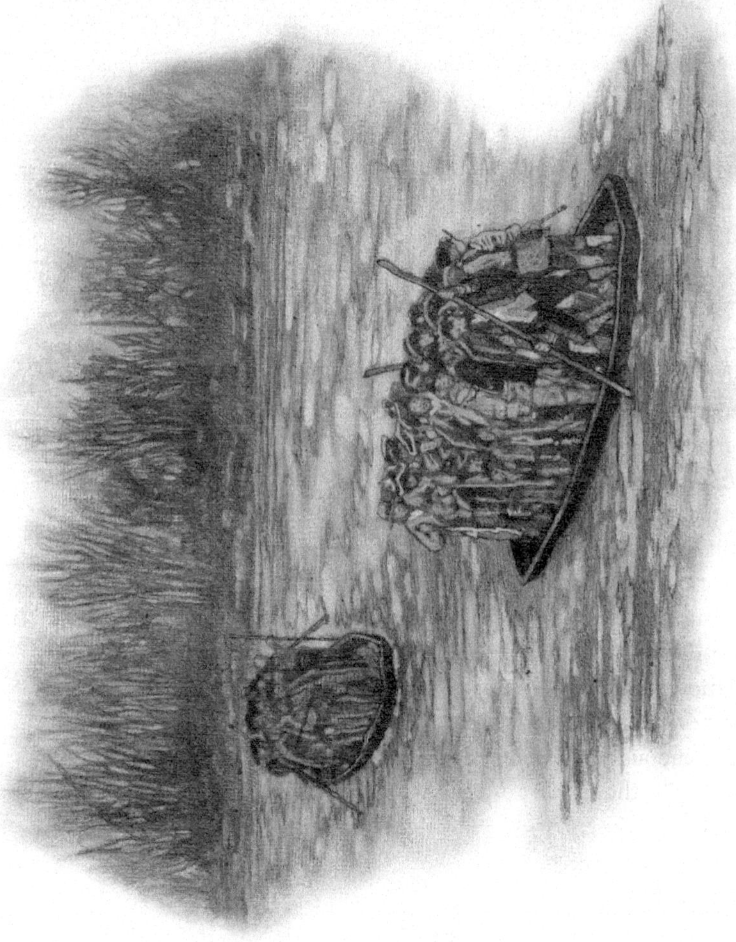

Patriot forces crossing a river. Nathanael Greene used the rain-swollen rivers of North Carolina to elude the British army under Cornwallis during the "Race to the Dan." Illustration by Stephen Marchesi.

suffered from hunger and plundered the countryside, while desertions increased. Under these conditions, Cornwallis sought to defeat Greene once and for all.

***February 25, 1781* (sometimes dated to February 23 or 24)**

Pyle's Defeat (also known as Pyle's Massacre or Haw River). Skirmish in Orange (modern Alamance) County. Dr. John Pyle, a Loyalist militia colonel in command of some 400 men, was surprised by Lee's Legion near the Haw River. Lee's men, at the head of Pickens's column, were mistaken by the Loyalists to be Tarleton's men, who were similarly uniformed down to the green jackets worn by both units. Lee was aware that the other force was made up of Loyalists, and he and his men rode among them. What happened next is a matter of controversy, including exactly how Lee planned to capitalize on this advantage. In some accounts, Patriot militia under Joseph Graham, following behind Lee's troops, recognized that they were among Loyalists and attacked them; in others, a Loyalist recognized that the newcomers were not from Tarleton's Legion and opened fire. Regardless, Lee and his men immediately responded to the initial outbreak of violence and began sabering and riding down Pyle's men, killing ninety-nine, wounding 150 others, and routing the rest, including Pyle. The Patriots suffered no casualties. Lee and Pickens, who had arrived on the scene, gathered up as quickly as possible Lee's men who had gone in pursuit of the survivors and resumed their march. Later in the day, a handful of the Loyalist wounded were killed by a unit of Catawba Indians under a Patriot officer who were passing through the area, while a few Loyalist prisoners were murdered by Lee's men that evening, supposedly in retaliation for Buford's Massacre at Waxhaws the previous May. Along with the news that Greene had returned to North Carolina, Pyle's Defeat had a tremendous negative impact on Loyalist morale and did much to cost Cornwallis the support of Loyalist recruits in the days leading up to Guilford Courthouse.

Ca. March 1781

Skirmish at Rouse's Tavern, near Wilmington, N.C. In the aftermath of his seizure of Wilmington, British Maj. Gen. James Craig attempted to suppress Patriot support in the surrounding area. The major Patriot military presence in the area was a militia force under Brig. Gen. John Alexander Lillington. On an unknown date, believed to have been sometime in March 1781, Lillington dispatched a party of twenty-five horsemen under Maj. James Love to gather up cattle in the area to prevent their falling into the hands of Craig's foragers. Craig and a small portion of this command spent an evening drinking at Alexander Rouse's Tavern and slept there. They were attacked in the early morning hours by British cavalry. Love and all of his companions were killed, excepting one who escaped.

March 1, 1781

The Articles of Confederation went into effect following ratification by all thirteen states.

March 2–3, 1781

Skirmish at Clapp's Mill in Alamance County. Otho Williams sent a force under Henry Lee to scout Cornwallis's movements on March 2. The command included Lee's Legion, Capt. Joseph Graham's company of mounted riflemen, and a company of Catawba Indians. Lee encountered Tarleton at Clapp's Mill in northwestern Alamance County. Both sides suffered light casualties after an exchange of gunfire lasting some fifteen minutes, resulting in Lee's withdrawal. On the following day, Lee sent Graham to investigate if Tarleton was still in the vicinity. After finding Tarleton's camp, Graham waited until sunset was approaching and sent a small party to notify Lee of what he had found and then advanced in an effort to capture some sentries. The latter became aware of the Patriot presence and a short fight followed, resulting in the capture of a British officer (*Note:* some accounts date the March 2 skirmish to March 4).

March 6, 1781

Skirmish at Weitzel's Mill, N.C. (also Whitesell's and several other spellings). Following the clashes in the vicinity of Clapp's Mill, Tarleton set out in pursuit of Lee, forcing Williams towithdraw his entire force and march to join Greene. A rearguard action was fought at Weitzel's Mill near Rocky Ford on the Reedy Fork Creek tributary of the Haw River on March 6, between Lee and Tarleton. It involved both mounted troops and infantry, with Tarleton also supported by four artillery pieces. Williams's command reached the creek first. He deployed militiamen from South Carolina, Georgia, and Virginia on the south side to cover the crossing of the Continental units. The British reached the field and were driven back by a volley from the Virginia riflemen posted south of the creek. The Continentals then formed line of battle and provided covering fire for the militiamen to cross in turn. A British infantry brigade under the command of Lt. Col. James Webster forced a crossing of the creek under heavy fire and drove back the Patriot right flank. Meanwhile, the British artillery deployed on the south side of the creek and opened fire, causing many of the militiamen who made up the Patriot infantry to flee. The remaining Patriots retreated. Although casualties were relatively light on both sides, the clash led to many of the militiamen from other states to go home, angry because they had been deployed to cover the retreat of the Continentals across the creek. In addition, Greene had dismounted the militia and let their horses go due to foraging problems. In the case of the South Carolina militiamen under the command of Andrew Pickens, Greene assigned them to operate under the command of Thomas Sumter in their home state. The departure of part of the militia deprived Greene of additional manpower shortly before Guilford Courthouse.

March 9–May 10, 1781

Siege of Pensacola, West Florida (modern Florida). Gov. Bernardo de Gálvez of Spanish Louisiana left Havanna, Cuba in February with a large expeditionary force to Pensacola, where he would be reinforced by more men from New Orleans and Mobile. Gálvez' force included Spanish regulars (including a regiment of exiled Irishmen), militiamen (including free Blacks from Cuba), and French regulars, supported by a Spanish and French fleet. His opponent, Maj. Gen. John Campbell, commanded a force of British and German regulars and Loyalist militiamen, along with Indian allies. Campbell surrendered on May 10. He also surrendered all of West Florida to Gálvez, a major setback to the British. The two-year campaign along the Gulf Coast had also prevented the detachment of British forces from West Florida to support operations in Georgia and the Carolinas (Mississippi Valley and Gulf Coast Campaign).

March 12, 1781

Greene marched to Guilford Courthouse and encamped.

March 15, 1781

The Battle of Guilford Courthouse, the largest and most important Revolutionary War clash fought in North Carolina. Greene's army numbered over 4,000 men, of whom some 1,700 were Continental regulars, and the rest were North Carolina and Virginia militiamen. Cornwallis's force numbered just over 2,000. Greene also took advantage of his examination

The Battle of Guilford Courthouse was the largest and most important of the Revolutionary War battles fought in North Carolina. Cornwallis finally caught up with Greene's army and attempted a decisive clash to destroy the Continental Army in the South once and for all. Greene arranged his force in successive lines, similar to Morgan's deployment at Cowpens. Cornwallis attacked and drove back the first two Patriot lines, but the fighting became more intense at the third line. Eventually Greene was forced to withdraw, but Cornwallis's army lost twenty-seven percent of its numbers in killed and wounded, wrecking its effectiveness. Painting by Don Troiani courtesy of Bridgeman Images.

of the terrain during his earlier encampment at Guilford Courthouse in making his battle plans. Cornwallis, who had also visited the area earlier, seems not to have done so. Taking his cue from Morgan at Cowpens, Greene arranged his forces into three successive battle lines, with the first two lines consisting mainly of militia bolstered by small contingents of Continentals. The bulk of the Continentals occupied the third line. The shakier militia were instructed to fire one volley at the advancing British, then withdraw. Action opened early in the morning at New Garden Meeting House, some miles south, when Lee, sent to delay the British advance, encountered Tarleton. Cornwallis's army did not reach the Patriot positions near Guilford Courthouse until around noon, allowing the Patriots time to eat, rest, and prepare. The battle started in the early afternoon, when the British drove toward the first and then the second Patriot lines. The main fighting occurred when the British assaulted the third line. Although outnumbered, the British veterans eventually drove the Patriots from the field after a stiff fight; the latter retired in good order. In the process, however, the British lost nearly 27 percent of their force killed and wounded, wrecking the effectiveness of Cornwallis's command and making the battle a truly pyrrhic victory for the British.

March 17, 1781

Dutch Guiana (modern Guyana), comprised of three small colonies, surrendered to the British.

March 18–September 8, 1781

Following Guilford Courthouse, Cornwallis marched toward Wilmington, where his army could resupply and reorganize for future operations. Greene followed but was unable to catch his opponent. Well aware that he would be unable to successfully attack Cornwallis in the Wilmington defenses, Greene made the decision to march into South Carolina and clear out the British garrisons there. He also hoped that Cornwallis would eventually follow. In a series of battles, Greene gradually pushed the British out of the interior, leaving them in control of only the major ports of Charleston, Wilmington, and Savannah.

March 18, 1781

Cornwallis began to march his troops to Cross Creek, where he hoped his troops would be resupplied from Wilmington and he could recruit among the largely Loyalist population of Highland Scot settlers.

March 21, 1781

Greene's army began its pursuit of Cornwallis.

March 27, 1781

Two thousand British and Hessian reinforcements under Maj. Gen. William Phillips, sent by Clinton from New York, arrived at Portsmouth, Virginia. Phillips superseded Arnold as commander of the British forces in Virginia.

April 1, 1781

Cornwallis arrived at Cross Creek and was disappointed to find that no supplies had been brought up from Wilmington. Very few of the local Highlander Loyalists enlisted to serve.

April 6, 1781

Greene abandoned following Cornwallis and began his march to South Carolina.

April 7, 1781

Cornwallis and his men arrived at Wilmington.

April 18–May 9, 1781

Following his instructions from Clinton to disrupt the flow of supplies from the North into the Carolinas to Greene, and to be in a position to better cooperate with Cornwallis, Phillips and 2,500 men sailed up the James River from Portsmouth on April 18, landed on the 19th, and captured Williamsburg and Yorktown. On April 25, Phillips defeated a force of 1,000 Virginia militia under the command of Maj. Gen. Baron Frederick von Steuben, who had been left by Greene in Virginia to oversee the movement of supplies to his army, at the Battle of Blandford. Phillips then occupied Petersburg on the same day. Steuben withdrew to Richmond, where his militia united with a force of 900 Continentals under the command of Maj. Gen. Marquis de Lafayette. Phillips reached Richmond on April 30, but on seeing Lafayette's force on the heights above the city, decided not to attack and sailed downriver. Receiving a letter from Cornwallis instructing him to move to Petersburg to await him there, Phillips complied and arrived on May 9. He soon fell ill and died of typhus.

April 25, 1781

While refitting his army in Wilmington, Cornwallis began to plan a new strategy which was at odds with his instructions from Clinton. He decided to shift his operations from the Carolinas to the Chesapeake area, where he would be reinforced by British troops already operating there under Benedict Arnold. Initially, Cornwallis was unaware of Phillips's arrival in Virginia. On learning of it, he used it to justify his decision, writing to Phillips that his own force was too battered to be of much use in South Carolina, but if united with Phillips in Virginia, they could accomplish much. On April 25, he began to march northward from Wilmington, initially keeping contact with Wilmington on the chance that word of a setback might arrive from South Carolina that would force a reluctant return southward after all. Clinton, meanwhile, would not learn of Cornwallis's decision until after he arrived in Virginia.

April 25, 1781

On the same day that Cornwallis started for Virginia, and that Phillips defeated Steuben near Petersburg, Nathanael Greene's army fought a major action against British forces at Hobkirk's Hill, South Carolina, just north of Camden. Greene's opponent was Lord Francis Rawdon, an able commander whom Cornwallis left in charge of British forces in the state when he marched into North Carolina. Rawdon, although outnumbered, advanced and broke the Continental line, forcing Greene to withdraw.

May 6–11, 1781

A series of skirmishes initiated by various Patriot forces attempted to slow Cornwallis's march to Virginia. On May 6, Col. James Gorham, with a force of some 400 Pitt County militiamen, tried to contend the crossing of Contentnea Creek at Peacock Bridge in Wayne (modern Wilson) County. Tarleton, commanding Cornwallis's vanguard, routed them. On the following day, Capt. Harry Hill and a detachment of Franklin County militiamen tried to block the march twice in Nash County, first at Swift Creek and then at Fishing Creek. In both cases, they were driven off by Tarleton. Arriving at Halifax later in the day, Tarleton was again confronted by militia defending a bridge, but he circled around and struck them from behind. The militia withdrew to a redoubt across the Roanoke River and fired on the British outside the town over the next four days, finally driven away when attacked by British infantry. Cornwallis then marched into and occupied the town. His men, angered by the resistance, sacked Halifax, and order was restored only with difficulty.

May 9, 1781

Rawdon abandoned Camden and marched to Monck's Corner. Despite the victory at Hobkirk's Hill, the British could no longer hold Camden as Greene remained in the area, supported by South Carolina militia forces under the command of Brig. Gen. Thomas Sumter. In addition, Col. Henry Lee and Francis Marion raided the British supply lines running from Camden to Charleston. Thus, Rawdon moved back.

May 13, 1781

Having heard word of Rawdon's victory at Hobkirk's Hill, and convincing himself that British control of South Carolina was no longer threatened, Cornwallis crossed the Roanoke River at Halifax and continued northward toward Virginia.

May 13, 1781

Two skirmishes fought near Legat's Bridge (also known as Rockfish and Legget's Bridge) between the command of Loyalist Capt. David Fanning and two different Patriot forces. In the first clash, Fanning surprised the camp of Capt. John Fletcher, whom Fanning had learned was gathering men to strike Fanning. In the second, Fanning encountered a group of men discharged from service under Col. Guilford Dudley who were on their way home from Greene's army being escorted by a force of dragoons. Fanning, riding ahead of his men stationed in ambush, bumped into Dudley's column and fled, with the dragoons in pursuit. They were routed when they fell into Fanning's trap.

May 20, 1781

Cornwallis and his army arrived at Petersburg, Virginia, and he assumed command of all British forces in the state. Arnold soon departed for New York. Additional reinforcements from New York intended for Phillips soon arrived, boosting Cornwallis's army to over 7,000 men. Cornwallis reviewed Clinton's instructions to Phillips, which had directed him to establish a naval base and conduct raids to disrupt the passage of supplies to Greene, and immediately abandoned plans for a major offensive in Virginia. What followed would be a frustrating spring and summer for both Cornwallis and Clinton. The commander-in-chief gradually revealed his anger regarding Cornwallis making an unauthorized move into Virginia and gave contradictory orders as to whether or not Cornwallis should dispatch a significant part of his army back to New York, which was under threat from the combined armies of Washington and the Comte de Rochambeau, or to be used in vaguely planned attacks against Philadelphia or Rhode Island. Although initially acting to comply, Cornwallis kept his army intact after Clinton abruptly canceled his orders for the detachment in July.

May 22–June 6, 1781

Patriot forces under Brig. Gen. Andrew Pickens and Col. Henry "Light Horse Harry" Lee successfully besieged Augusta, Georgia, occupied by Loyalist troops under the command of Lt. Col. Thomas Brown. Following the Loyalist surrender, Pickens and Lee reinforced Greene at Ninety-Six.

May 22–June 18, 1781

Nathanael Greene's army besieged the Loyalist forces occupying Ninety-Six, South Carolina, under the command of New York Loyalist Lt. Col. John Cruger. The garrison was relieved when Rawdon marched from Charleston to their support, forcing Greene's withdrawal. The British and Loyalists then abandoned Ninety-Six and withdrew to Charleston.

May 24–June 16, 1781

Cornwallis moved from Petersburg to disperse Lafayette's command and seize or destroy as many Patriot supplies as possible. Lafayette, who could do little with the forces at his disposal to stop Cornwallis, abandoned Richmond but attempted to concentrate to defend Fredericksburg, Cornwallis's intended target. Cornwallis, however, shifted westward and drove to the James River, sending detachments to hit major Patriot supply depots. One of these striking forces, under Tarleton, rode to Charlottsville, where the Virginia legislature had gathered after the abandonment of Richmond, and nearly captured the members of the assembly and Gov. Thomas Jefferson. Lafayette sone received a reinforcement of Continental troops under the command of Brig. Gen. "Mad" Anthony Wayne, and although still outnumbered, marched toward Cornwallis's encampment on the James. The latter withdrew to Richmond.

May 24–June 2, 1781

A French squadron commanded by Rear Adm. Comte de Grasse, recently arrived at Martinque, captured the British-held island of Tobago. De Grasse received dispatches from George Washington and Comte de Rochambeau, who commanded the French army in Rhode Island that recently marched south to join Washington. They requested that he sail to either New York City or Chesapeake Bay to assist in proposed operations against Clinton in New York or Cornwallis in Virginia. De Grasse, mindful that he needed to be back in the West Indies by October, opted for the latter, closer target, which influenced subsequent American and French campaign planning.

June 23–July 14, 1781

The General Assembly met at Bloomsbury (the Wake County Courthouse). As Abner Nash asked not to be reelected, Thomas Burke was chosen to be the third state governor of North Carolina.

June 26, 1781

Skirmish at Spencer's Ordinary [Tavern], Virginia. Cornwallis soon abandoned Richmond and marched to Williamsburg, arriving on June 25. Lt. Col. John Simcoe, of the Queen's Rangers had been assigned to screen Cornwallis's flank while raiding for Patriot supplies and ships along the Chickahominy River. Lafayette sent a force of Pennsylvania Continentals, Virginia riflemen, and dragoons under Col. William Butler to destroy Simcoe's command before it could reach Williamsburg. Simcoe's outnumbered men held off Butler's attacks and withdrew, and soon was united with the rest of Cornwallis's army. Both sides claimed victory.

July 4–August 18, 1781

Under new orders from Clinton to establish a post either at Yorktown or Williamsburg and send the rest of his army to New York City, Cornwallis departed Williamsburg on July 4, intending to cross the James River at Jamestown and then move on to Portsmouth, from whence he would send part of his army to Clinton. Cornwallis decided that, while he still had his army intact, he would try for a decisive clash with Lafayette. The opposing sides fought near Green Spring Plantation on July 6, where the British ambushed Lafayette's advance guard, which escaped after a hard fight. Cornwallis afterwards crossed the James and dispatched Tarleton on another raid directed at Patriot supply depots.

Thomas Burke was chosen as third governor of the state of North Carolina by the General Assembly in the summer of 1781. A previous delegate to the fifth North Carolina Provincial Congress and the Second Continental Congress, Burke was captured by Loyalist raiders under David Fanning in September at Hillsborough. Imprisoned on James Island near Charleston, he escaped in January 1782 and returned to North Carolina. Artist unknown, Thomas Burke, State Archives of N.C.

By late July, Cornwallis was in Portsmouth, where he received new orders from Clinton cancelling the call for the transfer of his troops to New York and was instead instructed to find another port to fortify as a naval station that was at a better and healthier location than Portsmouth. Clinton recommended either Old Point Comfort or Yorktown. Cornwallis deemed the former unsuitable and decided on Yorktown, fortifying it and Gloucester Point on the opposite side of the York River and moving his army to those locations in mid-August. Meanwhile, de Grasse's decision to sail from the West Indies to Virginia led Washington to abandon plans to attack Clinton in New York and instead to march south with his and Rochambeau's armies to trap Cornwallis.

July 17, 1781

Skirmish at Chatham Court House. By the summer of 1781, Maj. James Craig, commander of the British garrison at Wilmington, had promoted David Fanning to the rank of colonel and placed him over the Loyalist militia forces of Chatham and Randolph Counties. Hearing word that several Loyalist militia officers had been tried and scheduled to be hung at Chatham Courthouse on July 17, Fanning and a force of some fifty Loyalists surrounded the courthouse and struck on the morning of the scheduled hangings. They rescued the Loyalist prisoners and captured a number of Patriots. Most Patriots were immediately paroled, but a small number were turned over to Craig in Wilmington.

July 29, 1781

Skirmish at Alston House (the House in the Horseshoe) in Cumberland (modern Moore) County. Loyalist partisan Col. David Fanning attacked the home of Patriot militia Col. Philip Alston. Alston and his men had just returned from a raid and were asleep on the porch or in the vicinity of the house when the raiders struck in the morning. Alerted to the presence of the Loyalists by sentries, the militiamen barricaded themselves in the house, and a shootout followed. Alston decided to surrender when Fanning's men rolled a burning cart toward the house with intention of setting it afire. Alston's wife, Temperance, volunteered to negotiate surrender terms with Fanning, probably because a woman emerging from the building would have been less likely to have been shot outright by the Loyalists. She succeeded, and Alston and his men were paroled.

July 30, 1781

Skirmish at Cox's Mill, Randolph County. The mill was Fanning's base of operations. In his absence due to his raid on the Alston House, Patriot militiamen attacked the camp. They halted and retreated after receiving word that the Loyalists were returning.

August 1781

Maj. James H. Craig led an expedition from Wilmington into the interior with the object of punishing all those in the vicinity who refused to take an oath of loyalty to George III. The homes of many who refused to swear allegiance to the Crown were burned. A skirmish occurred with Patriot militia on August 2 at Rockfish Creek on the borders of Duplin and New Hanover (now Duplin and Pender) Counties and on August 17 at Webber's Bridge on the Trent River on the borders of Jones and Craven Counties. From August 19 to 21, Craig occupied New Bern, destroying the plantations of wealthy Patriots, liberating enslaved persons, and destroying ships at the docks. Departing on August 21, Craig skirmished with Patriot militia at Kingston (modern Kinston), but soon afterward heard rumors that reinforcements to Greene were headed from Virginia under the command of Gen. Anthony Wayne, and he withdrew to Wilmington. The rumors proved to be premature, however, as Wayne would not come further south until early in the following year.

August 3–4, 1781

A series of skirmishes between Patriot militiamen under Col. Thomas Wade and various Loyalist forces. The first occurred on August 3 at Piney Bottom Creek in Cumberland (modern Hoke) County, when Loyalist militiamen attacked Wade's camp. The Patriots were routed and six men were killed, as well as a boy who tended to the militiamen's wagons. Wade gathered the survivors and called for reinforcements. His command caught up with the Loyalists on the night of August 4 at Beatti's Bridge over Drowning Creek on the borders of Bladen and Richmond (now Scotland and Hoke) Counties. The Loyalists withdrew after the two sides exchanged fire in the dark. Wade continued his operations until August 9, seeking revenge for his dead men and in particular for the boy murdered by the Loyalists. Several Loyalists were taken prisoner and killed by the Patriots, including some who had not been involved in the Piney Bottom Creek skirmish.

August 28, 1781

Skirmish at Fanning's Mill on Little River in Montgomery County. A band of seventy Loyalists under Col. Hector McNeil surprised Patriot militiamen and captured some of them. He was subsequently pursued by a 400-man militia force led by Col. Thomas Wade.

September 1, 1781

Skirmish at Little Raft Swamp (also known as McPhaul's Mill and Burnt Swamp) in Bladen (modern Hoke) County. Col. David Fanning learned of Wade's pursuit of McNeil following the Fanning's Mill skirmish and came to the latter's support with a force of about 155 men. The combined Loyalist forces set a trap for Wade near Beatti's Bridge. After a prolonged skirmish, Wade, although his force outnumbered the Loyalists, withdrew. Fanning's plan to entrap the entire Patriot force failed, though they captured some.

September 5, 1781

The Battle of the Capes. A major naval clash near the mouth of Chesapeake Bay between de Grasse's French fleet from the West Indies and a British squadron from New York City under Rear Adm. Sir Thomas Graves. The British were driven off, and Graves returned to New York. De Grasse continued on to the Chesapeake, where he was reinforced by the French fleet from Newport, Rhode Island, under the command of Rear Adm. Comte de Barras. He sealed off access to the Chesapeake, made contact with Lafayette, and assisted in transporting the armies of Washington and Rochambeau to the York Peninsula.

September 8, 1781

Battle of Eutaw Springs, South Carolina. Maj. Gen. Nathanael Greene and his army, consisting of Continental units (including the 1st, 2nd, and 3rd Regiments of the North Carolina Continental Line, having been reorganized and recruited afresh after the capture of the original units at Charleston) and assorted units from the North and South Carolina militias, fought a mixed British and Loyalist force under the command of Lt. Col. Alexander Stewart, who replaced Rawdon when the latter left for Britain in July due to ill health. The battle was fought some sixty miles northwest of Charleston, near Nelson's Ferry on the Santee River. The British halted the initial Patriot attack and then counterattacked. They broke through the North Carolina Continentals, who although new were well-trained by Greene and fought well but lacked bayonets. The Maryland and Virginia Continental advanced, halted Stewart's men, and counterattacked in turn. The British camp was overrun. Stewart, however, rallied his forces near a brick house at the corner of the camp. Many of Greene's men meanwhile left the ranks and began to plunder the enemy camp. Other Patriot forces attempted to capture the brick house, but the British got there first, barricaded the building, and used it as a strong point to fire upon the Patriots. British troops positioned inside a thicket of blackjack trees opened up on the Patriots, killing many of Greene's cavalrymen and capturing Lt. Col. William Washington, whose horsemen had played key roles at Cowpens and other fights. A final British counterattack drove Greene's army from the field, but Stewart's army was so badly damaged that he had to withdraw to Monck's Corner and subsequently Charleston. Both sides claimed the battle as a victory, although Stewart lost nearly half his army as killed or wounded. The clash was the last major battle in the Carolinas.

September 12, 1781

Loyalist leader David Fanning surprised and captured Governor Burke and much of the General Assembly at Hillsborough. The Assembly still tried to meet in November but could not make a quorum and went home. The speaker of the state Senate, Alexander Martin, was appointed "acting governor."

September 13, 1781

An attempt by Brig. Gen. John Butler and a force of North Carolina militia to rescue Governor Burke failed when he intercepted Fanning's force at Lindley's Mill on Cane Creek in Orange County. Fanning's Loyalists defeated the militiamen after a fight of several hours, but Fanning was severely wounded in the process. Casualties were heavy on both sides. The Loyalists withdrew with their prisoners and eventually reached Wilmington.

September 28–October 19, 1781

The Siege of Yorktown. Cornwallis only became aware of his growing predicament in mid-September. He decided to attack to break out before he was completely hemmed in, but upon hearing word that Clinton planned to send reinforcements, opted instead to stay put in Yorktown. By September 28, Washington and Rochambeau had Yorktown under siege, while de Grasse continued to blockade the Chesapeake. Unable to escape or receive reinforcements, the latter of which were not sent until too late, Cornwallis surrendered his force of 7,000 men on October 19. The loss of so many men proved to be the final straw in Britain's attempt to subdue America. At war not only with the United States but with France, Spain, and the Netherlands, with British interests threatened in the Caribbean, at Gibraltar, and in India, and with West Florida already lost to Spain, Britain was not in a position to send reinforcements to America itself. Negotiations for a peace settlement was the only option, although it would take time for the British government to acknowledge this.

October 15, 1781

Skirmish at Raft Swamp in Bladen (modern Robeson) County between Patriot forces under Maj. Joseph Graham and Loyalists under Col. Duncan Ray. The Loyalists were routed.

On October 19, 1781, Cornwallis surrendered his besieged army at Yorktown to the combined Patriot-French army under the overall command of Washington. The surrender marked the beginning of the end of the conflict, as the loss of Cornwallis's army was a blow from which the British could not recover. Cornwallis himself refused to participate in the surrender ceremony, claiming to be ill, and sent Brig. Gen. Charles O'Hara to surrender the army on his behalf. Washington in turn delegated Maj. Gen. Benjamin Lincoln to receive O'Hara's sword. John Trumbull, 1820, Rotunda of the U.S. Capitol., accessed February 26, 2026, https://commons.wikimedia.org/wiki/File:Surrender_of_Lord_Cornwallis.jpg

November 18, 1781

The British evacuated Wilmington by sea. Craig and his men sailed to join the British forces in Charleston. Patriot militia under the command of Brig. Gen. Griffith Rutherford soon occupied the town.

November 26, 1781

A French force captured the former Dutch island of St. Eustatius from the British. The French returned the island to the Dutch in 1784.

November 27, 1781

Two days after the news of Yorktown reached London, George III addressed Parliament and revealed his intentions to carry on the war until victory.

December 10, 1781

Skirmish at Cox's Mill in Randolph County, when Patriot forces under Col. Elijah Isaacs captured Loyalist Col. David Fanning's main camp while the latter was away.

January 16, 1782

Gov. Thomas Burke escaped his confinement at James Island and made his way back to North Carolina. He attempted to reconvene the General Assembly on January 25 at Salem, North Carolina, but they did not reach a quorum.

January 19, 1782

A small force under the command of Anthony Wayne was dispatched by Greene to campaign in Georgia. On this date, Wayne crossed the Savannah River and entered Georgia.

January 29-February 5, 1782

A French expedition captured the former Dutch Guiana colonies from the British. They were returned to the Dutch in 1784.

February-March 1782

In late 1781, Capt. Thomas Shirley of the HMS *Leander*, accompanied by several transports carrying British soldiers, departed from England on an expedition to capture Dutch trading posts on the western coast of

Africa, along what was then known as the Gold Coast (modern-day Ghana). These posts traded mainly in enslaved persons and in ivory brought in from the interior. Shirley's initial foray against the Dutch post of Elmina on February 15-20 was unsuccessful, but later attacks from March 2-30 secured for the British several major posts. The loss of these posts posed a blow to the Dutch economy, and a gain for Britain's. The posts were returned to the Dutch under the 1784 Peace of Paris that ended the fighting between the two nations.

February 27, 1782

In London, the House of Commons voted to end military operations against the United States by nineteen votes.

March 20, 1782

Following a Parliamentary vote of no confidence in his leadership in the wake of Yorktown, Lord North resigned as Prime Minister and was replaced by William Petty Fitzmaurice, 2nd Earl of Shelburne, who oversaw the peace negotiations with America.

April 4–17, 1782

A British naval expedition from Charleston, carrying Loyalist Militia, raided Beaufort, North Carolina, in the last major military operation in the state. They landed on April 4 and occupied and sacked the town. They were opposed by elements of the North Carolina militia, who besieged the invaders. The Loyalists withdrew to their ships on April 6 but remained in the harbor until April 17.

April 15–May 18, 1782

The General Assembly convened in Hillsborough. It elected Alexander Martin as North Carolina's fourth governor.

May 1782

Clinton, recalled to Britain in the wake of the Yorktown disaster, was formally replaced as commander-in-chief of British forces in North America by Sir Guy Carleton, Governor-General of Canada.

July 11, 1782

British forces evacuated Savannah, Georgia.

Alexander Martin, fourth governor of the state of North Carolina. Accessed February 26, 2026, https://commons.wikimedia.org/wiki/File:NCG-Alexander Martin.jpg

November 30, 1782

In Paris, American and British representatives agreed after months of negotiations on a draft of a peace treaty that recognized American independence. The final version of the treaty, approved by both governments, was not signed until September of the following year, but as similar but separate drafts were made with the governments of France and Spain, military operations were at an end. It would take months for the news to reach some areas, so fighting continued in different parts of the world between the British and French, Spanish, and Dutch forces.

December 14, 1782

The British evacuated Charleston, South Carolina, ending their presence in the Southern states.

April 2, 1783

Shelburne was forced to resign as Prime Minister by a coalition led by Lord North and radical Whig politician Charles James Fox. He was replaced by William Cavendish-Bentinck, 3rd Earl of Portland, the last Prime Minister with even a nominal claim of authority over North America south of Quebec province, although Fox and North were the real powers within the resulting coalition government.

April 18–May 17, 1783

The General Assembly convened in Hillsborough. It reelected Alexander Martin as governor and formed two new counties, Greene and Davidson (both now in Tennessee).

May 17, 1783

The General Assembly passed "An Act of Pardon and Oblivion," which offered amnesty to all Loyalists except members of five designated classes.

June 7–29, 1783

The Siege of Cuddalore, India, part of the Second Anglo-Mysore War. The last battle of the American Revolutionary War, fought before the signing of the final major peace treaties in September. A force of British regulars, British East India Company troops, and Indian recruits battled a joint French and Mysorean command for control of a key port in the Bay of Bengal. The struggle ended inconclusively, as word finally reached the combatants of the preliminary peace treaties agreed upon the previous November. No Americans participated in the fight, which was strictly an Anglo-French-Indian colonial affair. However, the clash vividly illustrates how a war can spiral into many different directions as war aims expand, as well as the role that the strains on British military resources due to global warfare played to prevent them from concentrating their forces in America to defeat the revolutionaries.

September 3, 1783

The Treaty of Paris was signed, ending the war and formalizing America's independence. Two separate treaties were signed at Versailles on the same day, ending hostilities between the British and the French and the Spanish, respectively. Fighting continued between the British and the Dutch, and the British and the Indian state of Mysore (neither allied with the United States). A preliminary treaty had been signed between Britain and the Dutch Republic on September 2, but the final treaty was not signed until May 20, 1784, in Paris. The Treaty of Mangalore ended the Second Anglo-Mysore War on March 11, 1784.

Part V

From Confederation to Constitution, 1783–1789

Following eight years of war, the United States was an independent nation. Yet much remained unsettled, as both the national and the individual state governments faced many important issues in the peacetime world. These included the fate of the western lands long claimed by the colonial and state governments since the end of the Seven Years' War and which had been greatly added to in the wake of the Patriot victory. Relations between the states, between the states and the national government, and between the national government and its foreign counterparts were also an issue, as the weaknesses of the Confederation government became increasingly apparent. A movement rose to reform the national government, and a convention of representatives from the thirteen states met in Philadelphia in 1787 to revise the Articles of Confederation. The convention was called by individuals who, in fact, wanted to replace the Articles with a stronger governing document. After many debates and compromises, the convention adopted a new document, the Constitution, to replace the Articles. Sent to the states for ratification, the Constitution was the result of many compromises between those who advocated a strong national government and those who advocated some continuing form of federalism, a balance between the national government and the state governments. Those who preferred the weaker national government of the federation, with its much stronger role for the individual states, gradually coalesced into a movement called the Anti-Federalists. They opposed the adoption of the Constitution. Supporters of the Constitution then drafted a series of measures that consisted of a "bill of rights," which set further limits on the national government and made clear that all powers not specified as belonging to the national government were held either by the state governments or by the people themselves. Ten of these measures were passed by Congress and included as amendments to the Constitution. The Constitution was ratified by a majority of the states and went into effect in 1788, setting up the first national elections for president and for members of the new two-house congress. North Carolina, along with Rhode Island, did not participate in these elections, as both states were out of the union for having voted against acceptance of the Constitution. Following the establishment of the new national government, however, both states debated adoption of the Constitution again and decided in favor of it.

The establishment of the new national government under the Constitution marked an ending of sorts to a phase of American history that had begun with the first protests against Parliament's postwar taxation policies in 1763. In just twenty-six years, the Americans had moved from loyal, if protesting, citizens of the British Empire into an independent people with a nation of their own. While North Carolina had not often been in the forefront of these changes, its people played an important role in the events of the era and provided the setting for some of the most important developments in the Southern campaign, which ultimately undid British efforts to regain control of North America. During the postwar period, its political leaders and people robustly debated what sort of country they wished to belong to, at first rejecting the new Constitution until further guarantees of individual rights were offered. Ultimately affirming its place as a part of the United States, North Carolina and its people continued to participate in the challenges that the new nation faced in the decades ahead.

October 1783

A session of the General Assembly was called to meet in Hillsborough, but due to the lack of a quorum it failed to enact any legislation.

November 25, 1783

The British evacuated New York City. Washington and the Continental Army marched into the city in the wake of their withdrawal.

April 10–June 3, 1784

The General Assembly met in Hillsborough. It created three new counties, Fayette, Moore, and Sampson.

April 19, 1784

In the Cession Act of 1784, North Carolina ceded its western territories to the Confederation Congress.

June 3, 1784

The General Assembly passed a law abolishing entail and primogeniture, making inheritances more equitable. The practice had long been criticized throughout the colonies and associated in the minds of Americans with the idea of aristocracy, so the movement to change inheritance laws was part of the expansion of rights throughout the nation in the post-Revolutionary era.

August 24, 1784

A convention was held in Jonesborough by representatives from three counties in modern Tennessee. They made plans to organize a new state from the ceded western lands.

October 25–November 26, 1784

The General Assembly met in New Bern. They repealed the act creating the county of Fayette, and it reverted to its former name of Cumberland County.

November 1784

The North Carolina General Assembly rescinded the Cession Act.

December 1784

Unaware that North Carolina had rescinded the Cession Act, the western state movement held a second convention, formally announcing their plans to organize a new state, to be called Franklin.

March 1785

The legislature of the "State of Franklin" met and chose John Sevier to be governor. The movement did not receive enough support to achieve statehood under the Articles of Confederation, so it began to act as an independent republic.

May 13, 1785

Richard Caswell became governor of North Carolina again.

June 1785

The General Assembly met in New Bern, but due to the lack of a quorum it failed to produce any legislation.

June 10, 1785

The Treaty of Dumplin Creek ceded much Cherokee territory to the "state of Franklin." It was not universally accepted among the Cherokee leadership.

November 19–December 29, 1785

The General Assembly met in New Bern. It created one new county, Rockingham.

July 10, 1786

Gov. Caswell appointed Abner Nash, Alfred Moore, Hugh Williamson, John Gray Blount, and Philemon Hawkins to represent the state at the Annapolis Convention, called by Alexander Hamilton to discuss trade issues between the states. The Convention was held from September 11 to September 14. The representatives of only five states attended: Virginia, New York, Pennsylvania, New Jersey, and Delaware. North Carolina was one of four states that chose representatives but failed to arrive in time to attend. The Convention is considered a prelude to the Constitutional Convention held in Philadelphia the following year.

August 1786–February 1787

Shay's Rebellion, in western and central Massachusetts. A political movement led by a number of individuals but that became identified with war veteran Daniel Shays. It arose due to a debt crisis in Massachusetts and state government taxation policies. Protesters against these policies began to organize, calling themselves the Regulators after the prewar movement in North Carolina. Initially the protesters used their numbers to shut down local courts where debt cases were being tried, but they later organized into military units. An attempt to capture the federal armory in late January was repulsed by militia, and the movement was soon after crushed. There is disagreement among historians as to the role that the rebellion played in efforts to reform the national government, which under the Articles of Confederation was relatively weak and had been unable to authorize funding for troops to put down the rebellion.

November 30, 1786–January 6, 1787

The General Assembly met in Fayetteville. They created three counties, Robeson, Hawkins, and Sumner (the latter two both now in Tennessee).

January 6, 1787

The General Assembly chose William R. Davie, Richard Dobbs Spaight, Gov. Richard Caswell, Alexander Martin, and Willie Jones to represent North Carolina at the Federal Convention in Philadelphia. Jones and Caswell declined to participate and were replaced by Hugh Williamson and William Blount.

May 25–September 17, 1787

The Federal Convention met in Philadelphia. Convened to discuss possible amendment of the Articles of Confederation, it instead produced an entirely new governing document, the Constitution, in place of the Articles. The Constitution was written after extensive debates over the nature of a new government, with competing plans offered regarding whether representation should be based on state population or on equal representation for each state. There was also a major controversy over whether or not enslaved persons should be included in the population count for representation. The plan of government that was eventually drafted involved a system of checks and balances between three branches of the national government, and between the national government and the states. The national government no longer consisted of a one-house Congress but of an executive branch, headed by an elected president; a two-house Congress, consisting of an elected senate on the basis of equal representation (two senators for each state), and a house of representatives elected on the basis of population; and an appointed supreme court. Enslaved persons, even though they were not free and could not participate in elections, did count for population representation persons, but not on a person-by-person basis. Instead, they were counted as "three-fifths" of a person. The "three-fifths" compromise gave the Southern states a disproportionate amount of power in the new house of representatives. Upon passage by the convention and its announcement to the public, the Constitution was sent to the states for ratification.

November 19–December 22, 1787

The General Assembly met in Tarborough.

November 26, 1787

The first recorded case in which a state law was declared unconstitutional, *Bayard v. Singleton* was a legal landmark, establishing the precedent of judicial review. It involved the daughter of a Loyalist whose lands and property had been confiscated under acts passed by the General Assembly during the Revolution and a more recent act passed in 1785, who sought to recover them from their current owner. A panel of judges meeting in New Bern decided that the 1785 law was unconstitutional and heard it on that basis, although they eventually decided in favor of the defendant based on a technicality.

December 6, 1787

The General Assembly called for the election of delegates to attend a convention for ratifying or rejecting the new United States Constitution.

December 20, 1787

Samuel Johnston became governor of North Carolina.

December 22, 1787

The legislature passed an act making the Treaty of Paris state law and ordering the state court system to follow its provisions when applicable. As there were clauses in the treaty prohibiting the confiscation of Loyalist property, this should have ended the practice, although in fact it did not always do so.

June 21, 1788

The United States Constitution was ratified by the minimum of states required for it to go into effect.

July 21, 1788

In Hillsborough, the ratifying convention convened. The majority of participants were Anti-Federalists, who argued against adoption of the Constitution until a bill of rights was presented to North Carolina. Their views prevailed, and by a vote of 184 to 83 the delegates declined to ratify the Constitution without the inclusion of a bill of rights. North Carolina and Rhode Island, which had voted against ratification in a popular referendum in March, were now outside of the Union under the Constitution.

September 13, 1788

The Confederation Congress passed a resolution for the Constitution to go into effect with the eleven states that had ratified.

September 30, 1788–January 22, 1789

The legislatures of the states held the first elections for the U.S. Senate (elections for the Senate by direct popular vote did not begin until November 1914, after the adoption of the Seventeenth Amendment to the Constitution in 1913). North Carolina, having not ratified the Constitution, did not participate.

November 3–December 6, 1788

The General Assembly met in Fayetteville. It formed two new counties, Iredell and Tennessee (the latter gave its name to the future state, and upon its formation became a part of it, dividing into the counties of Montgomery and Robertson).

November 24, 1788–March 5, 1789

The first elections for the House of Representatives were held, with election dates varying widely by state. North Carolina, having not ratified the Constitution, did not participate.

December 15, 1788–January 10, 1789

The first presidential election under the new Constitution was held. North Carolina, having not ratified the Constitution, did not participate. George Washington won the popular vote.

February 1789

Under increasing attacks from the Cherokee and other American Indian peoples, the "state of Franklin" collapsed and its remaining leaders swore allegiance to North Carolina.

March 4, 1789

The Constitution went into full effect as the new Congress met for the first time.

April 6, 1789

The United States Congress met to count the electoral votes for president. It affirmed that George Washington had been elected President.

April 30, 1789

George Washington was inaugurated as the first President of the United States.

September 28, 1789

The United States Congress passed twelve articles of amendment for consideration by the states, including those out of the Union. The articles were intended to collectively function as a bill of rights, guaranteeing certain powers to the states and their citizens. Ten were eventually ratified.

November 2–December 22, 1789

The General Assembly met in Fayetteville. They created one new county, Stokes.

November 21, 1789

A second North Carolina ratification convention met in Fayetteville. The passage of a bill of rights by Congress in September, and effective lobbying by Federalist advocates James Iredell and William R. Davie set the stage for passage, which came at a vote of 195 to 77. North Carolina was back in the Union.

Bibliography

Babits, Lawrence E. *A Devil of a Whipping: The Battle of Cowpens* (Chapel Hill: University of North Carolina Press, 1998).

Babits, Lawrence E. and Joshua B. Howard. *Long, Obstinate, and Bloody: The Battle of Guilford Courthouse* (Chapel Hill: University of North Carolina Press, 2008).

Billias, George Athan, ed. *George Washington's Generals* (New York: William Morrow, 1964).

Billias, Geore Athan, ed. *George Washington's Opponents: British General and Admirals in the American Revolution* (New York: William Morrow, 1969).

Black, Jeremy. *Crisis of Empire: Britain and America in the Eighteenth Century* (London: Continuum, 2008).

Boatner, Mark M., III. *Encyclopedia of the American Revolution* (New York: McKay, 1974).

Borick, Carl P. *A Gallant Defense: The Siege of Charleston, 1780* (Columbia: University of South Carolina Press, 2003).

Buchanan, John. *The Road to Charleston: Nathanael Greene and the American Revolution* (Charlottesville: University of Virginia Press, 2019).

Buchanan, John. *The Road to Guilford Courthouse: The American Revolution in the Carolinas* (New York: Wiley, 1997).

Butler, Lindley S. *North Carolina and the Coming of the Revolution, 1763–1776* (Raleigh, N.C.: Division of Archives and History, 1976).

Caldwell, William. "Isaac Shelby, Patrick Ferguson, and Fire & Sword: The Power of a Good Story," *Journal of the American Revolution*, posted May 28, 2024, https://allthingsliberty.com/2024/05/isaac-shelby-patrick-ferguson-and-fire-sword-the-power-of-a-good-story/.

Carpenter, Stanley D. M. *Southern Gambit: Cornwallis and the March to Yorktown* (Norman: University of Oklahoma Press, 2019).

Cecere, Michael. *The Invasion of Virginia 1781* (Yardley, Penn.: Westholme, 2017).

Cecere, Michael. *March to Independence: The Revolutionary War in the Southern Colonies, 1775–1776* (Yardley, Penn.: Westholme, 2021).

Crow, Jeffrey J. *The Black Experience in Revolutionary North Carolina* (Raleigh, N.C.: Division of Archives and History, 1977).

Crow, Jeffrey J. *A Chronicle of North Carolina during the American Revolution 1763–1789* ((Raleigh, N.C.: Division of Archives and History, 1975).

Denman, Jeffrey A. and John F. Walsh. *Greene and Cornwallis in the Carolinas: The Pivotal Struggle in the Company, 1780–1781*, (Jefferson, N.C.: McFarland and Co., 2020).

Dupuy, R. Ernest, Gay Hammerman, and Grace P. Hayes. *The American Revolution: A Global War* (New York: David McKay Company, 1977).

Fenn, Elizabeth A. *Pox Americana: The Great Smallpox Epidemic of 1775–82* (New York: Hill and Wang, 2001).

Ferling, John. *Almost a Miracle: The American Victory in the War of Independence* (New York: Oxford University Press, 2009).

Ferling, John. *Winning Independence: The Decisive Years of the Revolutionary War, 1778–1781* (New York: Bloomsbury, 2021).

Freeman, W. Trevor. "North Carolina's Black Patriots of the American Revolution" (master's thesis, East Carolina University, 2020). https://thescholarship.ecu.edu/server/api/core/bitstreams/ca1b1c9c-93b2-4484-99c-96e6ddf6d88e/content.

Ganyard, Robert L. *The Emergence of North Carolina's Revolutionary State Government* (Raleigh, N.C.: Division of Archives and History, 1978).

Glickstein, Don. *After Yorktown: The Final Struggle for American Independence* (Yardley, Penn.: Westholme, 2015).

Greene, Jerome A. *The Guns of Independence: The Siege of Yorktown, 1781* (El Dorado Hills, Calif.: Savas Beattie, 2005; paperback rprt., 2013).

Kierner, Cynthia A. *The Tory's Wife: A Woman and Her Family in Revolutionary America* (Charlottesville: University of Virginia Press, 2023).

Lee, Wayne E. *Crowds and Soldiers in Revolutionary North Carolina: The Culture of Violence in Riot and War* (Gainesville: University Press of Florida, 2001).

Maas, John R. *The Battle of Guilford Courthouse: A Most Desperate Engagement* (Charleston, S.C.: History Press, 2020).

Maas, John R. *The Road to Yorktown: Jefferson, Lafayette, and the British Invasion of Virginia* (Charleston, S.C.: History Press, 2015).

Mackesy, Piers. *The War for America, 1775–1783* (Cambridge: Harvard University Press, 1964).

Middlekaupf, Robert. *The Glorious Cause: The American Revolution, 1763–1789* (Oxford History of the United States volume 3, 1982; revised second edition, New York: Oxford University Press, 2004).

O'Kelley, Patrick. *Nothing But Blood and Slaughter: The Revolutionary War in the Carolinas*. 4 vols. (Trenton, Ga.: BookLocker.com, 2004–2005).

O'Shaughnessy, Andrew Jackson. *The Men Who Lost America: British Leadership, the American Revolution, and the Fate of the Empire*. (New Haven: Yale University Press, 2013).

Orrison, Robert and Mark Wilcox. *All That Can Be Expected: The Battle of Camden and the British High Tide in the South, August 16, 1780* (El Dorado Hills, Calif.: Savas Beattie, 2023).

Pancake, John S. *This Destructive War: The British Campaign in the Carolinas, 1780–1782* (Tuscaloosa.: University of Alabama Press, 1985).

Powell, William S. *The War of the Regulation and The Battle of Alamance, May 16, 1771* (Raleigh, N.C.: State Department of Archives and History, 1949; repr., 1976).

Rankin, Hugh F. *Greene and Cornwallis: The Campaign in the Carolinas* (Raleigh, N.C.: Division of Archives and History, 1976)

Rankin, Hugh F. *North Carolina in the American Revolution* (Raleigh, N.C.: Division of Archives and History, 1959).

Rankin, Hugh F. *The North Carolina Continentals* (Chapel Hill: University of North Carolina Press, 1971).

Robinson, Blackwell P., ed. *The Revolutionary War Sketches of William R. Davie* (Raleigh, N.C.: Division of Archives and History, 1976).

Simms, Brendan. *Three Victories and a Defeat: The Rise and Fall of the First British Empire* (New York: Basic Books, 2007).

Treacy, M. F. *Prelude to Yorktown: The Southern Campaign of Nathanael Greene, 1780–1781* (Chapel Hill: University of North Carolina Press, 1963).

Walker, Melissa. *The Battles of Kings Mountain and Cowpens: The American Revolution in the Southern Backcountry* (New York: Routledge, 2013).

Ward, Christopher. *The War of the Revolution*, ed. by John Richard Alden, 2 vols. (New York: Macmillan, 1952).

Waters, Andrew. *To the End of the World: Nathanael Greene, Charles Cornwallis, and the Race to the Dan* (Yardley, Penn.: Westholme Publishing, 2020).

Wickwire, Francis and Mary. *Cornwallis: The American Adventure* (Boston: Houghton Mifflin, 1970).

Wilson, David K. *The Southern Strategy: Britain's Conquest of South Carolina and Georgia, 1775–1780* (Columbia: University of South Carolina Press, 2005).

Notes